The
Peak District

AA Publishing

Produced by AA Publishing

First published 1997

Published by AA Publishing (a trading name of Automobile
Association Developments Limited, whose registered office is
Norfolk House, Priestley Road, Basingstoke, Hampshire RG24 9NY;
registered number 1878835).

ISBN 0 7495 1496 5

A CIP catalogue record for this book is available from the British
Library.

The contents of this book are believed correct at the time of printing.
Nevertheless, the publishers cannot be held responsible for any
errors or omissions or for changes in the details given in this book or
for the consequences of any reliance on the information provided by
the same. Material in this book has been previously published by
AA Publishing in various publications.

Designer: Stuart Perry

AA Publishing would like to thank Roland Smith, Head of Information
Services for The Peak National Park and Chairman of The Outdoor
Writers' Guild, and Richard Hankinson, Squire of Saddleworth
Morris Men, for their knowledge and assistance.
Features: 'The Peak District National Park' by Roland Smith, and
'The Saddleworth Morris Men and the Rushcart Procession' by
Richard Hankinson.

Colour separation by BTB, Digital Imaging, Whitchurch, Hampshire

Printed and bound by George Over Ltd, Rugby

THE PEAK DISTRICT

The Peak District, at the southern end of the Pennines, was designated Britain's first national park in 1951. It covers 555 square miles (1,438sq km) of Derbyshire and extends into five neighbouring counties. The Dark Peak peat moorlands fringed by gritstone 'edges' contrast with the deep limestone dales of the White Peak countryside. Surrounded by Manchester, Sheffield and other heavily populated areas, the Peak District has for many years provided an important and accessible area of countryside for town-dwellers. In the 1930s, this access was increasingly threatened by the exclusive use of the moors for grouse shooting, and several demonstrations culminated in a 'mass trespass' on to Kinder Scout on 24 April 1932, showing the strength of popular feeling, and helping to hasten the establishment of the national parks. The Peak National Park Authority has a responsibility to protect and enhance the landscape, to promote understanding and to provide recreational opportunities. It has pioneered planning and traffic management schemes, and the provision of courses at its own study centre, Losehill Hall, balancing the needs of visitors with those of the 38,000 people for whom the Peak District is home and workplace.

A restored water-powered scythe and steel works dating back to the 18th century, the hamlet retains its working water wheels as well as forging hammers, grindstones and the world's only surviving working Huntsman crucible steel furnace. Abbeydale is a magical place where the visitor can wander at will, viewing the Victorian manager's house and workman's cottage, watching local craftsmen at work in the workshops and contrasting today's tranquil atmosphere with Sheffield's rich industrial history. Telephone for details of the programme of exhibitions, special events and working days.

Open all year, most days. Closed Xmas and New Year.

An attractive village in the White Peak limestone area, where the rivers Lathkill and Bradford meet. The 18th-century cornmill with its wheel and five sets of millstones is still intact.

A hamlet with a largely Norman church, close to the Ashbourne to Buxton road, in good walking country; the Tissington Trail is close by. There are Bronze Age burial mounds, known locally as 'lows', on the surrounding hills.

Izaak Walton fished from a riverside house in this village where the River Dove winds through a dramatic ravine, with weirs, waterfalls and caves.

This attractive market town lies just south of the Peak District National Park, a good centre from which to explore Dovedale and the Manifold Valley. The cobbled market place is triangular, stretching up the hill along the road leading north to Buxton. The many outstanding Georgian buildings include almshouses, town houses and inns such as the Green Man and Blacks Head. The latter is no longer an inn, but it still retains its rare 'gallows' inn sign across the main street. The church, at the west end of town, described by novelist George Eliot as 'the finest mere Parish Church in England' has the tallest spire in the Peak District at 212ft (65m).

Today's visitors can enjoy traditional Ashbourne gingerbread, washed down with Ashbourne water drunk from a glass made from the local Derwent Crystal. On Shrove Tuesday or Ash Wednesday, all the streets are taken over by the traditional 'football' games, with hundreds of players on each side.

(See also Cycle ride: The Tissington Trail from Ashbourne to Hartington, page 78.)

ABBEYDALE
SOUTH YORKSHIRE
INDUSTRIAL HAMLET, ABBEYDALE RD SOUTH, 4 MILES (6.5KM) SW OF SHEFFIELD ON A621
TEL: 0114 236 7731

ALPORT
DERBYSHIRE. VILLAGE OFF B5056, 3 MILES (5KM) S OF BAKEWELL

ALSOP EN LE DALE
DERBYSHIRE. HAMLET OFF A515, 6 MILES (9.5KM) N OF ASHBOURNE

ALSTONEFIELD
STAFFORDSHIRE. VILLAGE OFF A515, 6 MILES (10KM) N OF ASHBOURNE

ASHBOURNE
DERBYSHIRE. TOWN ON A52, 13 MILES (21KM) NW OF DERBY

ASHFORD IN THE WATER

*T*his scenic ride through the heart of the Derbyshire Peak District tackles the hills on their easiest gradients and has only two sharp descents. There are magnificent views across high sheep pastures and into craggy, wooded dales. The local white limestone creates distinctive drystone walls and farmsteads in the hills, and charming cottages in the villages.

Cressbrook Mill was originally a cotton mill

INFORMATION

Total Distance
20 miles (32km), with 220yds (200m) off-road, 17½ miles (28km) using the two off-road short cuts or 13 miles (21km) using off-road short cuts and omitting Over Haddon.

Difficulty
Challenging

OS Map
Landranger 1:50,000 sheet 119 (Buxton, Matlock & Dovedale)

Tourist Information
Bakewell, tel: 01629 813227; local information displays at Tideswell Dale picnic area, Millers Dale Station, and Over Haddon Craft Centre.

Nearest Railway Station
Grindleford (Manchester/Sheffield line).

Refreshments
The Bulls Head, Ashford in the Water, a favourite cyclists' pub, has a room for children and sunny seats outside. At Great Longstone the Crispin Inn welcomes children and has a beer garden. The Monsal Head Hotel Stable Bar and Tea Room is open all day every day except Christmas, or you may prefer the Monsal View Café next door. Opposite the Millers Dale Station car park, the Wriggly Tin Café is open Friday 11–5, Sat/Sun 10.30–5, whilst

at Over Haddon, the Yew Tree Tea Room offers home baking every day of the week. There are picnic spots at Mondal Head and in Tideswell Dale.

START

Ashford in the Water is bypassed by the A6, 1½ miles (2.5km) north-west of Bakewell. Take the A6020 over the River Wye and go immediately left into the village. The small free car park is on the right in about ½ mile (1km). Millers Dale Station pay-and-display car park, on the Monsal Trail, provides an alternative start from the west.

At Litton Mill in Millers Dale

DIRECTIONS

1. Turn right out of the car park and immediately right again to climb gently to the B6465. Cross on to a narrow lane which rises through the tangled woods of Thornbridge Hall towards Longstone Edge and the village of Great Longstone.

2. Go left at the T-junction, past Longstone Hall, and climb again to recross the B6465 at spectacular Monsal Head. Descend with care to Upperdale for an idyllic ride on a single-track lane beside the River Wye.

3. At Cressbrook Mill there is a choice. For a short, flat route join a concessionary path, part of the Monsal Trail, by turning left through the second gateway (there are two stone balls on the

wall) and walking your cycle through lovely Water-cum-Jolly Dale for about 1 mile (1.5km), to join a narrow lane at Litton Mill leading to Millers Dale. Alternatively, continue on the road for 2 miles (3km) as it leaves the dale and winds up through woodland to emerge amongst hill pastures. Turn left and then left again at the junction on the outskirts of Litton down tiny Litton Dale, go left on the B6049 and climb slightly past the Tideswell Dale picnic area before swooping down to Millers Dale under a fine viaduct.

4. Over the river the road starts to rise, and around the corner is a further choice of routes. With low gears you can take part of the walkers' Limestone Way, a steep

tarmac byway on the left. This levels off to become a good stone and grass lane which joins the road towards Priestcliffe. For a gentler climb, remain on the B6049 for a further mile (1.5km) and go left towards Priestcliffe, ascending steadily to the A6. Cross the A6, turning left and immediately right (with care) through the outskirts of Taddington. Turn right at the crossroads and climb to the edge of Taddington Moor where The Jarnet offers a smooth descent. Turn left at the crossroads for a short climb on to High Low and views of the old Magpie Mine.

5. Past the mine entrance, at the

On the banks of the River Wye at Ashford in the Water

Ashford turn, is a short cut left, straight down Kirk Dale. Otherwise continue, and in ¼ mile (0.5km) take a broad stone track right to descend Bole Hill. At the crossroads take the tiny lane opposite along Mandale Rake and down to Over Haddon, perched on the hillside above Lathkill Dale. Immediately after the 30mph sign turn right into the hamlet. Follow the road round to the left in front of Yew Tree Tea Room and keep left, with views over the dale to the right, passing the Craft Centre and Information Office. As you leave the hamlet, the road dips and Bakewell and the eastern gritstone edges appear ahead. At the B5055 go right and soon left. Stay on this

quiet lane above the Wye Valley, as far as the T-junction.

6. Turn right for a thrilling descent of Kirk Dale and at the A6 go right and look for the old Sheepwash Bridge almost immediately on the left. Dismount

The Monsal Trail near Millers Dale by the River Wye

and cross the bridge into Ashford. Rejoin the road by the well and turn left; you will shortly see the car park on the right.

PLACES OF INTEREST

Ashford in the Water

This typical Derbyshire village retains many of its old customs. Five wells are dressed for Trinity Sunday and paper garlands of maidens who died before their wedding day hang in the church. There is an attractive information plaque, on the wall by the 17th-century Sheepwash Bridge.

(See also page 10.)

Cressbrook Mill

An impressive, partly ruined Georgian building, this was originally a cotton mill, taking water from the Wye to power two large waterwheels before steam turbines were introduced in 1890. Conditions at this mill were reasonable, but at Litton Mill pauper apprentices were cruelly treated and many children died.

The Monsal Trail

This long-distance trail uses part of the disused Bakewell/Buxton railway line, bought by the Peak National Park Authority in 1980. Only short stretches are currently suitable for cycling as several tunnels are closed. Information is provided at Miller's Dale Station for four mountain bike circuits using the trail and byways.

The Limestone Way

Following 26 miles (42km) of footpaths and lanes from Matlock to Castleton, this walker's trail is waymarked with the Derby Ram.

WHAT TO LOOK OUT FOR

Passing through Great Longstone note the village cross and attractive Crispin Inn sign. At Monsal Head stop and admire the breathtaking view of the dales and viaduct before you descend. Look for trout in the Wye and Lathkill rivers, and for the dipper, a shy little black and white bird which swims underwater. In Millers Dale note the large disused mill wheel; the river once supported 20 mills and works. Everywhere you can discover the remains of lead mining; grassy dips and hummocks and long rakes. Examination of almost any drystone wall will reveal carboniferous limestone fossils; fragments of crinoid stems, shells and corals, and sometimes fine crystals; transparent calcite, blue john and silver lead ore.

The Magpie Mine

With its ruined engine house, the Magpie Mine is a prominent relic of Derbyshire's lead mining past, accessible by footpath. Near by, Mandale Rake is a long scar from which a seam of lead has been extracted, and Bole Hill is the site of early lead smelting. Rakes and boles are frequently wooded to prevent livestock grazing the poisoned ground.

(See also page 10.)

Lathkill Dale

This nature reserve is one of Britain's best wildlife sites and well worth exploration. There is a concessionary footpath through the dale alongside the river and its mill pools, old lead mines, natural caves and cliffs. The old Ricklow Quarry spoil heaps, towards the dale head, are covered in wild flowers, including

A beautiful early spring orchid at Cressbrook Dale

the rare Jacob's Ladder. Visit the Information Room in Over Haddon Craft Centre for full details of the current flowers in bloom and of bird sightings.

(See also page 65.)

ASHFORD IN THE WATER
DERBYSHIRE. VILLAGE OFF A6, 2 MILES (3KM) NW OF BAKEWELL

Opposite: the medieval bridge at Bakewell

Two ancient bridges span the Wye in this delightful village, one dated 1664 and the other complete with a sheep-dipping enclosure at one end. An interesting well-dressing ceremony is held on the Saturday before Trinity Sunday. Ashford marble, popular in Victorian times (for vases, fire-surrounds etc) was quarried near by.

(See also Cycle ride : Ashford in the Water, page 6.)

ASHTON-UNDER-LYNE
GREATER MANCHESTER. TOWN ON A627, 6 MILES (9.5KM) E OF MANCHESTER

An industrial mill town in the foothills of the Pennines with its own canal. The Grade I Listed Church of St Michael and All Angels has a spectacular stained-glass window. At the Portland Basin Heritage Centre visitors can discover the social and industrial history of the Tameside area, while the Museum of the Manchesters tells the story of the Manchester Regiment.

Museum of the Manchesters
MARKET PLACE
TEL: 0161 342 3078

This is an interesting museum illustrating the history of the Manchester Regiment and its relationship with the local community, from the early 19th century to National Service. An extension follows the story of Women at War during World War I and World War II, and features an audio-visual presentation. There is also an exhibition on the history of medals, with examples from the Manchester Regiment on display.

Open all year, most days.

BAKEWELL
DERBYSHIRE. TOWN ON A6, 7 MILES (11KM) NW OF MATLOCK

A busy cattle market and the largest town in the national park, Bakewell stands on the wooded banks of the Wye and is sheltered by hills on three sides. Many of its attractive gritstone buildings bear witness to a historic past, and its beautiful 12th-century church is famous for the superb Saxon cross (English Heritage) preserved in its churchyard. The five-arched medieval bridge (English Heritage) was widened in the 19th century but is basically one of the oldest structures of its type in Britain. The Old Market Hall, which dates from the 17th century, is now the Peak National Park Information Centre. The name of the town will always be associated with the Bakewell pudding, apparently created by accident when a harassed cook in the Rutland Arms mistakenly poured the egg mixture meant for the pastry of a jam tart into the jam. The unusual dish was very well received by guests and the cook was instructed to continue making her delicious mistake.

Magpie Mine
SHELDON, 3 MILES (5KM) W OFF B5055
TEL: 01629 583834

The surface remains of the mine are the best example in Britain of a 19th-century lead mine. It was worked (unsuccessfully) in 1958, and then stabilised in the 1970s.

Open all year, daily. Closed Christmas.(See also Cycle ride: Ashford in the Water, page 6.)

BAMFORD

*DERBYSHIRE. VILLAGE ON
A6013, 2 MILES (3KM) NW
OF HATHERSAGE*

BASLOW

*DERBYSHIRE. VILLAGE ON
A623, 3 MILES (5KM) NE OF
BAKEWELL*

BEELEY

*DERBYSHIRE. VILLAGE ON
B6012, 5 MILES (8KM) N OF
MATLOCK*

*Sheep grazing by Baslow
Edge*

The village is pleasantly situated between the Hope Valley and Ladybower Reservoir, on the hillside above the River Derwent. Sheepdog trials are held during the late Spring Bank Holiday, and well-dressing ceremonies, when elaborate mosaic pictures are made from petals, leaves and bark, take place in July.

This characteristic gritstone village stands on the River Derwent and is partly built around the old triangular Goose Green. Most through traffic is taken across the river by a recent bridge, but the 17th-century hump-backed crossing with three arches survives complete with tollhouse. Nether End, on the far side of Baslow, marks the north entrance to the Chatsworth estate and has thatched cottages overlooking Bar Brook.

This estate village, largely laid out by Paxton, lies at the southern end of Chatsworth Park, below Beeley Moor. St Anne's Church has a Norman doorway and 13th-century chancel. A tributary of the River Derwent, which is famous for its trout, runs close to the village. Beside the inn a minor road climbs to Beeley Moor, where there are more than 30 prehistoric barrows and cairns.

(See also Chatsworth, page 27.)

Gazetteer

The village is close to beautiful Dovedale. Cyclists and walkers can approach along the Tissington Trail, a former railway route. Biggin Hall dates from 1672, and the Church of St Thomas from the 1840s. (See also Cycle ride: The Tissington Trail, page 78.)

Situated on the hillside of Stanton Moor, the village is built of warm local gritstone. In the 18th century a clergyman, the Reverend Thomas Eyre (died 1717) carved Rowtor Rocks into seats and caves; he also built Rowtor Chapel.

Bollington is a stone-built former cotton village. On nearby Kerridge Ridge is White Nancy, a folly which was built to commemorate the Battle of Waterloo (1815).

A former lead-mining and textile centre with a medieval stone cross on 1·3 circular stone steps standing in the former market place, and 17th-century limestone cottages. The Pig of Lead inn on Via Gellia reflects the local lead-mining industry. On a steep hill above the village is the Church of St James which dates from the 13th century.

BIGGIN
DERBYSHIRE. VILLAGE OFF A515, 8 MILES (13KM) N OF ASHBOURNE

BIRCHOVER
DERBYSHIRE. VILLAGE OFF B5056, 4 MILES (6KM) W OF MATLOCK

BOLLINGTON
CHESHIRE. TOWN ON B5090, 3 MILES (5KM) NE OF MACCLESFIELD

BONSALL
DERBYSHIRE. VILLAGE OFF A5012, 2 MILES (3KM) SW OF MATLOCK

*T*he route links the twin villages of High and Low Bradfield, idyllically set in a steep Pennine valley. Fine views of the surrounding moors, an interesting church and the story of the worst dam-burst disaster in British history make this a walk to remember.

Grid ref: SK262920

INFORMATION

The walk is 2 miles (3km) long. Mostly easy lane and field walking, with one steep climb. Several stone squeeze-stiles. Dogs should be kept on leads. There are pubs in both Low and High Bradfield

START

Low Bradfield is off the B6077, about 7 miles (11km) west of the centre of Sheffield. The walk starts from the car park on the western side of the village recreation ground.

DIRECTIONS

1. From the car park turn right, following the narrow path signed 'Path to High Bradfield', parallel to the stream on your right and a wall on your left. Turn right at the second footbridge, and up a steep flight of stone steps. At the top cross a track and climb five more steps. Keep ahead between a fence and a wall to reach the road.

2. Turn left along the road which leads up and alongside the wall of the Agden Reservoir. When the road curves around to the right, follow the footpath signed 'Bailey Hill', which winds steeply up to the right by the side of a plantation. Continue to climb up steeply until you reach a path junction by a stile on the right. Directly ahead and partly overgrown by trees is Bailey Hill, a Norman motte and bailey castle (no access).

3. Turn right over the stile and follow the path across to the churchyard, entering through two gates. Walk through the churchyard to the main gate, with the Watch House on your left. Keep forward into Towngate and into the hilltop village of High Bradfield.

4. Now turn right into Woodfall Lane, signed 'Low Bradfield and Dungworth'. Soon after the lane bends to the left, turn left at a stone stile following the public footpath signed 'Low Bradfield'. Keep to the edge of the field by a stone wall, and follow it as it curves right.

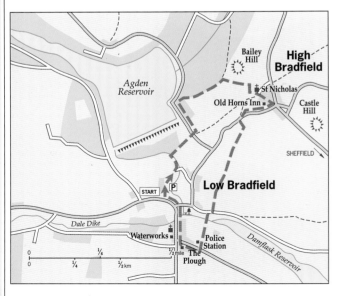

5. Continue across several walls and stiles to cross the fields, keeping a line of electricity poles 20yds (18m) to your right, and later descend another uneven flight of stone steps on to a lane (care needed) near the upper end of the Damflask Reservoir.

6. Cross the footbridge over the River Loxley almost opposite the steps, and continue along School Lane, which leads via a walled path to another lane, emerging by the police station. Turn right here back towards the village, and right again at the Plough pub into Mill Lee Road for the return to the car park.

PLACES OF INTEREST
St Nicholas Church
High Bradfield's lovely parish church, built mainly in the 15th century has fine views across the green dale with its many reservoirs to the moorlands beyond. The Gothic-style Watch House on the edge of the churchyard was built in the days when body snatching was rife.

The Bursting Dam Disaster
Just after midnight on 11 March 1864, the newly-completed Dale Dike Reservoir west of Low Bradfield burst its walls following a landslip. About 700 million gallons of water surged down Bradfield Dale and on as far as the outskirts of Sheffield. A mill at Low Bradfield was swept away and a total of 244 people died. Another 20,000 people were made homeless.

The Church of St Nicholas

WHAT TO LOOK OUT FOR

Despite their usual retiring nature, weasels are seen fairly regularly in the area, feeding among the stone walls. Watch for agitated meadow pipits perched on the stones. Foxes are sometimes observed crossing the open moors, which are the haunt also of red grouse.
The reservoirs harbour waterbirds in autumn and winter.

BRADWELL

Derbyshire. Village on B6049, 4 miles (6.5km) W of Hathersage

BRASSINGTON

Derbyshire. Village off B5056, 4 miles (6.5km) W of Wirksworth

BURBAGE

Derbyshire. Village on A53, on W outskirts of Buxton

Huddled below Bradwell Edge, this village was the birthplace of Samuel Fox, the inventor of the umbrella frame. Bagshawe Cavern, discovered by lead-miners in 1806, is near by, and offers adventure caving trips.

A former lead-mining village of grey stone, with some fine 18th-century houses and a Norman church. Below the village is Carsington Reservoir (known as Carsington Water) which offers a variety of recreational activities.

This former quarrying centre, now effectively a suburb of Buxton, is located below Grin Low Bronze Age barrow. On this stands Solomon's Temple look-out tower, a folly dating from 1896.

Butterton is a high moorland village close to the Manifold Valley. The Church of St Bartholomew, built 1871–3 by Ewan Christian, with a later spire, has an interesting 14th-century font.

Situated just outside the boundaries of the national park, this is the highest town in England and an ideal base from which to tour the moors and dales of the Peak District. It is sheltered by hills even higher than its 1,000ft (300m) site, yet is able to offer gentle scenery more typical of the lowlands alongside sedate reaches of the lovely River Wye. Grinlow Woods lie to the south of the town, Corbar Woods are a mere half mile (1km) away, and just east is the enchanting valley of Ashwood Dale.

BUTTERTON

STAFFORDSHIRE. VILLAGE OFF B5053, 6 MILES (9.5KM) E OF LEEK

BUXTON

DERBYSHIRE. TOWN ON A515, 18 MILES (29KM) NW OF ASHBOURNE

Buxton's Pavilion gardens are colourful in all seasons

The town itself is built round a spa whose medicinal properties were discovered by the Romans and exploited to the benefit of the town towards the end of the 18th century, when Buxton rivalled the elegant supremacy of Bath. The growth of the town during this period was largely due to the efforts of the 5th Duke of Devonshire, who built the beautiful Crescent and Pump Rooms opposite the town's hot springs. The pale blue mineral water of the area still bubbles up from a mile (1.5km) underground at a constant temperature of 82 degrees Fahrenheit (28

A fine view of Buxton, with its elegant Crescent

degrees Celsius) and now feeds the local swimming pool.

The River Wye runs through an attractive park overlooked by the 1870s iron and glass Pavilion Gardens conservatories, restaurants, and Octagon Hall. In 1979 the restored 900-seat Opera House in Buxton was re-opened and the Buxton Festival was founded. It takes place around the turn of July and August, and one of the festival's highlights has always been the performance of neglected operas. Each year a fresh theme is chosen, concentrating on the influence of a creative artist on his own time and on subsequent generations, and the festival's major events are linked with this theme. The Devonshire Royal Hospital was originally built as the Great Stables and has a superb dome that was added in 1870.

Poole's Cavern (Buxton Country Park)
GREEN LANE
TEL: 01298 26978

The natural limestone cavern lies in 100 acres (40.5ha) of woodland. The cave is 1,000ft (305m) in length, with only 16 steps, making it suitable for all ages. There is a conducted tour with a guide that takes about 40 minutes. It is rich in beautiful formations which include thousands of stalactites and stalagmites. An exhibition of artefacts from the cave dig, covering the Stone Age to Roman times, also includes the story of limestone and a display of British minerals and fossils.

Open Mar–Oct, daily.

CAPESTHORNE HALL
CHESHIRE. 5 MILES (8KM) W OF MACCLESFIELD
TEL: 01625 861221 & 861779

The Bromley-Davenports can trace their ancestry back to the Norman Conquest, and their ownership of the Capesthorne estate was recorded in the Domesday Book. The present house, dating from the early 18th century with substantial Victorian alterations, replaced a timber-framed building on the site. Although even its owners are reluctant to call it beautiful, with its blackened towers and pinnacles above the red-brick façades, it has immense character; it is also packed with all kinds of treasures.

Fire damage in 1861 resulted in substantial rebuilding of parts of the house by the great Victorian architect Anthony Salvin

Much of the charm of Capesthorne lies in its variety. There are sumptuous state rooms – the dining room is particularly striking – which contrast with such rooms as the delightful American Room, furnished in colonial style from the Philadelphia home of the present Lady Bromley-Davenport. There is the Dorothy Davenport Room, with its splendid Jacobean four-poster bed, and the state bedroom, containing the chairs used by the family at the coronation of Queen Elizabeth II. The material on the bedhead is the same as that used at Westminster Abbey. Fine classical marbles and busts adorn the sculpture gallery, and beneath it all the cellars have various displays and exhibitions, including an array of Civil War armour.

Surrounding the hall are beautiful gardens and grounds, with lakes and woodland walks. Various fairs and open air concerts take place each season; please telephone for details.

Open Mar–Oct, selected days.

The industrious Dame Dorothy Davenport (1562–1639) spent 26 years completing the needlework for the great four-poster bed in the room now named after her

CASTLETON

DERBYSHIRE. VILLAGE ON A625, 5 MILES (8KM) W OF HATHERSAGE

Beautifully situated at the head of the Hope Valley, Castleton shelters beneath the Norman ruin of Peveril Castle (English Heritage) and is overlooked by Mam Tor, topped by a Bronze and Iron Age hillfort and known as the 'Shivering Mountain' because of its instability.

Traffic leaves the valley by spectacular Winnats Pass, a narrow limestone gorge. These hills are the unique source of Blue John, a fluorspar whose attractive purplish veining is seen in huge vases and urns at many historic houses and at the village's Ollerenshaw Collection. Pendants, brooches and ear-rings are produced from the smaller quantities of Blue John mined today from Treak Cliff Cavern.

Special interest holidays can be enjoyed at the Peak National Park's Study Centre at 19th-century Losehill Hall.

Secluded Cave Dale, south of Castleton

Castleton celebrates Oak Apple Day (29 May) with its 'Garlanding' ceremony, which attracts huge crowds with much music and merrymaking. A procession is led by the 'King' and 'Queen' in costume and on horseback. Accompanied by a silver band they visit local pubs, girls dance and everyone welcomes the summer.

South of Castleton is Cave Dale, a beautiful secluded valley with a winding path and streams.

(See also Walk: Castleton and Cave Dale, page 24.)

The cavern is a remarkable example of a water-worn cave, and measures over a third of a mile (0.5km) long, with chambers 200ft (61m) high. It contains eight of the 14 veins of Blue John stone, and has been the major source of this unique form of fluorspar for nearly 300 years.

Open all year, daily. Closed 25–26 Dec & 1 Jan.

Blue John Cavern
BUXTON RD
TEL: 01433 620638

This is one of the most spectacular natural limestone caves in the Peak District, and has a well-lit underground walk. Ropes were made for over 500 years in the 'Grand Entrance Hall', and traces of a row of cottages can be seen.

Open Etr–Oct, daily.

Peak Cavern
ON A625
TEL: 01433 620285

William Peveril, one of William the Conqueror's most trusted knights, guarded the King's manors in the Peak District from this natural vantage point. The castle is now in the care of English Heritage. Today's visitor is greeted with spectacular views across the Hope Valley and beyond, and the meadow above the village is designated a Site of Special Scientific Interest.

Open all year, most days. Closed 24–26 Dec & 1 Jan.

Peveril Castle
MARKET PLACE
ON S SIDE OF CASTLETON
TEL: 01433 620613

Visitors descend 105 steps to a boat which takes them on a 1-mile (1.5-km) underground exploration of the floodlit cavern with its 'Bottomless Pit'.

Open all year daily. Closed 25 Dec.

Speedwell Cavern
OFF A625, ½ MILE (1KM)
W OF CASTLETON
TEL: 01433 620512

Discover the rich deposits of the rare and beautiful Blue John stone and fine stalactites and stalagmites on a guided tour of the caverns, which are illuminated by spectacular lighting and have safe footpaths. The Dream Cave, Aladdin's Cave, Fairyland Grotto, the Seven Dwarfs, the Fossil Cave, the Dome of St Paul's, the Witches Cave and the 'Pillar' – the largest piece of Blue John ever found – are all seen in the quarter of a mile (0.5km) tour which lasts about 40 minutes.

Open all year, daily. Closed 25 Dec.

Treak Cliff Cavern
¾ MILE (1KM) W ON A625
TEL: 01433 620571

*T*his is an easy exploration of the best of Derbyshire's limestone country, centred on the busy tourist village of Castleton, with its famous caves and castle. The walk climbs up the rocky gorge of Cave Dale, then descends steeply back to the village.

Grid ref: SK149829

INFORMATION

The walk is 2 miles (3km) long.
Involves some steep sections.
Several gates, stiles and cattle grids.
Dogs should be kept on leads.
Pubs and cafés in Castleton.
Picnic places in Cave Dale.
Toilets at car park.

START

Castleton stands at the head of the Hope Valley on the A625 Sheffield to Chapel-en-le-Frith road. Park in the large village car park (pay-and-display) in Cross Street.

DIRECTIONS

1. From the car park, turn left along Cross Street, passing the Town Ditch on the left. In a few yards, at The Castle pub, turn right (Castle Street). Passing the church on the left, enter the Market Place. Turn left to pass the war memorial into Bargate, then in 50yds (45m) turn right, signposted 'Limestone Way'. Cross a wooded stile where the rock walls narrow, and start the climb up through the dale (Peveril Castle stands high on its precipitous crag above you to the right). Follow this path to a metal gate near the head of the dale, where the gradient eases. Now

The view from Peveril Castle, high above Castleton

keep a drystone wall on your right and later pass through a metal gate. At the next metal gate, turn sharp right into a walled green lane which leads over the hill. (Cave Dale is now visible to the right, and on reaching the crest of the hill, the face of the 'Shivering Mountain' of Mam Tor is on the left.)

2. Pass through an old metal gate and keep ahead, descending more steeply now. At the foot of the hill pass through a gate on to a walled lane, with Goosehill Hall on your left, to re-enter Castleton at Goosehill Bridge. Afterwards keep left to walk down the footpath beside Peakshole Water, which issues from the huge mouth of Peak Cavern. On reaching the main road, turn into Cross Street, with the car park almost opposite.

PLACES OF INTEREST

Caves and crags
Castleton is at the heart of an area where streams sink suddenly beneath the porous white limestone rock into the spectacular caves which have been formed by this water erosion over the years. Many of the caves are open to the public. Peak Cavern, in the village, has the largest cave entrance in Britain and once housed a community of rope makers.

Speedwell Cavern, at the foot of the Winnats Pass, is entered by

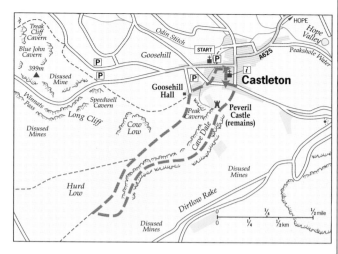

boat on an underground canal cut by lead miners; the Treak Cliff and Blue John Caverns in the hills to the west have the best displays of the rare semi-precious stone Blue John, which is not found anywhere else in the world. The craggy gorges of Cave Dale and the Winnats Pass are thought to have been formed when swift currents of meltwater from Ice Age glaciers cut through the 300 million-year-old reef limestone. (See also page 22.)

Blue John stone

WHAT TO LOOK OUT FOR

The grassy slopes of the Derbyshire Dales are rich in flowers, including early purple orchid, cowslip, bird's-foot trefoil and common rock-rose. On some of the steeper slopes, particularly below crags, is the rare limestone polypody fern. Butterflies include orange tip, green hairstreak and common blue. The woods are home to chaffinches, willow warblers, wood warblers, spotted flycatchers, and great spotted and green woodpeckers.

CHAPEL-EN-LE-FRITH

DERBYSHIRE. TOWN OFF A6, 5 MILES (8KM) N OF BUXTON

Magnificent Chatsworth

A market town on the border of the Peak District National Park, whose name means 'chapel in the forest'. The chapel, consecrated in 1225, and expanded in the early 14th century with some later alterations, is dedicated to St Thomas à Becket. There is a 17th-century market cross in Market Place; most of the notable buildings are Victorian. Otters and owls are bred at the Chestnut Centre Conservation Park.

gazetteer

This palatial home of the Dukes of Devonshire, which sits splendidly in the Derwent Valley, is one of the grandest and best-loved of the stately homes in Britain. The first house at Chatsworth was built by Bess of Hardwick, Countess of Shrewsbury, a remarkable lady who had four husbands and grew substantially richer and more powerful with each widowhood. At Chatsworth she was with her second husband, Sir

CHATSWORTH
DERBYSHIRE. 1½ MILES (2.5KM)
S OF BASLOW
TEL: 01246 582204

The Cascade in the park at Chatsworth

William Cavendish, and they began building here in 1552, although the development of the house continued over many years.

In 1686 the 4th Earl, who was created 1st Duke of Devonshire in 1694, began to demolish parts of it to make way for new buildings designed by Thomas Archer. He also rebuilt the west front and lived just long enough to see completed the supremely beautiful house which delights visitors today. Only the chapel, the state dining room and the sculpture gallery remained as they were originally built.

Marble statuary from the 1st century AD in the north entrance hall and the painted ceiling panel provide a hint of the glories to come, but few visitors are prepared for the breathtaking painted hall, with the whole of the ceiling and upper walls covered with scenes from the life of Julius Caesar, painted by Louis Laguerre in 1692. Amidst all this splendour, the estate children's Christmas party takes place every year, and the knowledge of this adds a delightful human touch to the beautiful but inanimate features.

The series of state rooms continues in equally grand style, suitably furnished and adorned with fine works of art and magnificent Mortlake tapestries. In the state music room there is also a touch of humour in the form of a *trompe-l'oeil* painting of a violin on an inner door which really does deceive the eye, even at very close quarters.

The bed in the state bedroom originally belonged to King George II, and on his death it was presented to the 4th Duke. King George V and Queen Mary slept here when they stayed at Chatsworth for the Royal Show at Derby in 1933.

The Oak Room is the oldest room in the house, with oak panelling and carved heads from a German monastery, one of the many purchases made by the 6th Duke. An avid collector of art and classical works, he was just one in a long line of Cavendishes who have shaped this splendid house and filled it with wonderful things.

In 1939 a girls' school was relocated to Chatsworth. Assemblies were held in the painted hall, physics was taught in the butler's pantry, art in the orangery, biology in the still room and chemistry out of harm's way in the stable block. There were dormitories all around the house, and 20 girls slept in the state drawing room.

The park is one of the finest in Britain. It was laid out by 'Capability' Brown, but is most famous as the work of Joseph Paxton, who became head gardener in the 19th century. Notable features include the newly-restored Cascade and the Emperor Fountain, which sends up a jet of water to 290ft (88m). Other attractions are the farming and forestry exhibition and the adventure playground. Guided tours are available at extra cost. Special events are held throughout the year.

Open late Mar–late Oct, most days.

CHELMORTON

DERBYSHIRE. VILLAGE OFF A5270, 4 MILES (6KM) SE OF BUXTON

Chelmorton is the second highest village in the country. Stone walls enclose narrow fields behind farms which line the village street up to the church. Well-dressings take place here, usually in June.

CHESTERFIELD

DERBYSHIRE. TOWN ON A61, 10 MILES (16KM) S OF SHEFFIELD

The crazily twisted 228-ft (69-m) lead-covered spire of St Mary and All Saints' Church is Chesterfield's best-known landmark; the twisting is caused by the use of unseasoned timber. The large and fascinating church beneath has fine monuments to the Foljambe family from 1510.

The heart of the town is the popular open market, established for 800 years, and claimed to be England's largest. The Market Square narrowly escaped total change in the 1970s. Wiser counsel prevailed, however, traditional frontages were retained, and the Pavements Shopping Centre constructed behind to maintain the town's role as a major shopping centre.

The 16th-century timber-framed former Peacock Inn, now the tourist information centre, and other jettied Tudor buildings confirm Chesterfield's long history, but the black-and-white timbering in Knifesmithgate is a 1930s whim, inspired by Chester. The impressive red-brick town hall opened in 1938.

Chesterfield's 16th-century Revolution House

Chesterfield's industrial development owed much to George Stephenson, who lived at Tapton House and is buried at Holy Trinity Church. Leisure facilities include Queen's Park Sports Centre, the Pomegranate Theatre, the Museum and Art Gallery telling the story of Chesterfield, the Winding Wheel entertainment centre, annual well-dressings, and numerous special events.

A mill town which rose to prominence in the Tudor period when it prospered in lace-making and leather-working, and later in the silk and cotton industries. One of the most impressive buildings in the town is the Venetian Gothic town hall. To the east is the Cloud, the penultimate peak of the Pennine chain, which is visible for miles around. The Bridestones are the remains of a chambered tomb thought to have been built in the Stone Age.

This large village has a hilltop church and market cross, and gritstone cottages leading downhill to where the street broadens beside a solidly-built chapel. The National Tramway Museum was developed in a former quarry beneath Crich Stand, the inland lighthouse monument to the Sherwood Foresters Regiment.

This unique 'action stop' offers a scenic journey through a period street to open countryside with panoramic views. Visitors can enjoy unlimited tram rides. The exhibition hall houses the largest national collection of vintage electric trams from home and abroad. Other attractions include a video theatre, shops, café, a playground and picnic areas. There is plenty to see and do, both indoors and out. Special events are held during the year. Please telephone for dates.

Open Apr−Oct, most days.

The world's first cotton-spinning mill was built here by Richard Arkwright in 1771. The mill, which is open to visitors, now houses displays, craft shops and a restaurant. Willersley Castle, once Arkwright's home is now a Methodist holiday centre. A fine old bridge that spans the River Derwent here carries a rare 15th-century bridge chapel (English Heritage).

(See also Walk: Cromford Canal, page 32.)

Sir Richard Arkwright established the world's first successful water-powered cotton mill at Cromford in 1771. The Arkwright Society is involved in a major restoration project to create a lasting monument to an extraordinary genius.

Open all year, daily. Closed 25 Dec. Guided tours.

CONGLETON
CHESHIRE. TOWN ON A54, 11 MILES (18KM) N OF STOKE-ON-TRENT

CRICH
DERBYSHIRE. VILLAGE ON B5035, 4 MILES (6KM) N OF BELPAR

National Tramway Museum
*MATLOCK RD
(OFF B5035)
TEL: 01773 852565*

CROMFORD
DERBYSHIRE. VILLAGE ON A5012, 2 MILES (3KM) N OF WIRKSWORTH

Cromford Mill
*MILL LANE
TEL: 01629 824297*

CROMFORD CANAL

*E*xplore Derbyshire's industrial heritage, from the site of Richard Arkwright's first cotton mill, along a beautifully-restored canal, and back through delightful woodland.

Grid ref: SK302569

INFORMATION

The walk is about 3½ miles (5.5km) long.

First part, along canal towpath, easy; return more strenuous.

Several squeeze-stiles.

Dogs should be kept on leads, except in Cromford Meadows.

Picnic area in Cromford Meadows, near the start; also at High Peak Junction.

Pubs and cafés in Cromford.

Toilets at Cromford Meadows.

START

Cromford Wharf and Meadows are just off the A6, 18 miles (29km) north of Derby and 3 miles (5km) south of Matlock Bath. There is plentiful parking on Cromford Meadows and at the High Peak Junction.

DIRECTIONS

1. From Cromford Wharf, set out south along the towpath, signed 'High Peak Junction', with the canal on your right. Follow the towpath for just over a mile (1.5km) to reach High Peak Junction. There is a choice of routes here.

(The shorter alternative is to cross the Derwent at High Peak Junction by the footbridge, signed 'Holloway', and walk up the lane towards Lea Bridge, where you meet the longer route at * below.) The main walk continues for about ¼ mile (0.5km) to the Lea Wood Pump House, crossing the

Derwent by an aqueduct and then turning left over the railway tunnel entrance on the path through Lea Wood to reach Lea Bridge*. At the road turn left and cross the bridge, then branch right through a squeeze-stile into a wood. Follow the main path, bearing left through this pleasant mixed woodland.

2. Eventually emerge on to a green lane and at the fork, keep right on a well-defined path. Continue across four fields and

Arkwright's Cromford Mill, built in 1771

hrough a wood. At the far end continue to a crossways and turn eft to descend to the road, oining it under the railway oridge. Pass Cromford Station and the entrance to Willersley Castle (private). Carefully cross Cromford Bridge to return to the car park.

PLACES OF INTEREST

Cromford Canal

Built to serve Richard Arkwright's Cromford Mill (the first water-powered cotton mill in the world), the Cromford Canal was opened in 1793. It was used for the transportation of cotton and other goods until the coming of the railway in the 1860s. The 5½-mile (9-km) stretch between Cromford and Ambergate has been restored.

Lea Wood Pump House

This distinctive building, with its classically-shaped chimney, was built in 1840 to pump water from the nearby River Derwent into the canal. It houses the original steam-powered beam engine, currently under restoration by enthusiasts. It is open to the public on some summer weekends.

Sir Richard Arkwright and Cromford

Richard Arkwright transformed textile manufacturing from a cottage industry to a factory operation, and his first mill, the fortress-like Upper Mill near the

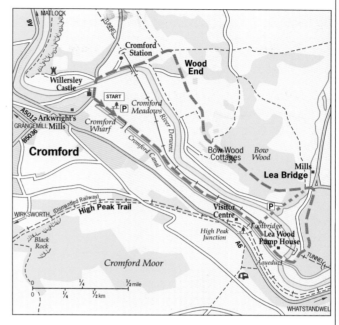

start of the walk, was built in 1771. It now includes a visitor centre. At the height of its production the mill employed 500 workers, many of whom lived in Arkwright's model village of Cromford, and many of his cottages still survive. He amassed a great personal fortune, but he died in 1792, just before the completion of his stately country

house, Willersley Castle (private), near the end of the walk.

(See also page 31.)

WHAT TO LOOK OUT FOR

The Cromford Canal is a haven for wildlife, with a profusion of wild flowers including blue water-speedwell, water mint, forget-me-nots and marsh marigolds. Birds include mallard, coot, moorhen and, if you are lucky, the occasional kingfisher, while small mammals which may be seen include water shrews and water voles.

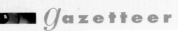
DARLEY DALE
DERBYSHIRE. HAMLET ON A6, 3 MILES (5KM) NW OF MATLOCK

Situated alongside the River Derwent, Darley Dale is linked to Matlock by the restored Peak Railway. Stone from Stancliffe Quarry, long prized as building and sculpting material, was used for the flagstones in Trafalgar Square.

DELPH
GREATER MANCHESTER. VILLAGE ON A62, 4 MILES (6.5KM) NE OF OLDHAM

Delph is a pretty village in Saddleworth, whose name comes from the Old English word for quarry. Castleshaw Fort, above the village, was one of a series of forts constructed by the Romans and built on the road between Chester and York.

DERBYSHIRE DALES
DERBYSHIRE. SCENIC REGION

Dramatic limestone gorges, wooded dales, picturesque villages and market towns in the southern part of the Peak District National Park.

DERWENT, RIVER
RISES NEAR GLOSSOP AND JOINS THE TRENT

From the Peak District moors above Glossop, the river flows through valleys which were flooded to create the Derwent Reservoirs and the attractive villages beneath gritstone edges, past the magnificent house of Chatsworth, and through Matlock Bath's limestone gorge to Cromford, where Arkwright harnessed its power for cotton-spinning, fuelling the Industrial Revolution. The Derwent passes Belper's mills, and flows on through the city of Derby, before joining the River Trent at Sawley.

DOBCROSS
GREATER MANCHESTER. VILLAGE OFF A670, 4 MILES (6.5KM) E OF OLDHAM

Dobcross is a village of some interest for the social historian and industrial archaeologist. It grew up in the 18th century at the junction of two packhorse routes in the Pennine foothills, and until about 1850 was the commercial and social heart of the Saddleworth weaving district. It has survived intact, its austere, dark gritstone buildings a perfect reflection of developments in the woollen trade at the time. An expansion in the domestic weaving industry locally led to the building of cottages with purpose-built rooms for the workers' looms, usually on the second floor, and there are a number of these houses in Dobcross, clearly distinguished by the long rows of stone-mullioned windows that provided the necessary light. The tall, terraced weavers' cottages and larger clothiers' and merchants' houses line the narrow streets and stand haphazardly in the cobbled square at the top of the village. The square has changed little in 200 years. Around it can also be seen a range of warehouses, a row of shops dated 1789, the 18th-century Swan Inn and the former Saddleworth Bank building of 1813.

Dobcross was the birthplace of the giant textile machinery business, Platt Brothers. It was on the strength of prosperity such as theirs that the village church was built in 1787, in the unpretentious style of a preaching house. More recently, the village has been used as the setting for the film *Yanks*.

Opposite:
Dobcross, once home to the weaving industry

gazetteer

DOVEDALE

*DERBYSHIRE/STAFFORDSHIRE.
VALLEY 4 MILES (6.5KM) NW
OF ASHBOURNE, OFF A515*

EARL STERNDALE

*DERBYSHIRE. VILLAGE OFF
B5053, 4 MILES (6.5KM) SE
OF BUXTON*

EDALE

*DERBYSHIRE. VILLAGE OFF
A625, 5 MILES (8KM) NE OF
CHAPEL-EN-LE-FRITH*

*Picturesque Dovedale is
popular with walkers*

Situated within the National Trust's South Peak Estate, Dovedale is a popular and accessible beauty spot. A broad level path follows the east bank of the river past craggy rocks and pillars, dense woodland, dark caves and cascading waters.

A Peak District quarrying village near Buxton, whose Quiet Woman inn has a headless woman on its sign. The 19th-century Church of St Michael was rebuilt in the 1950s after war damage.

Edale in the valley of the River Noe, is a dairy- and sheep-farming area made up of ancient farming communities, called the Booths, which have grown into hamlets. The village, which has two hotels, a Peak National Park Information Centre, camping facilities, accommodation, and a youth hostel is the last stop before the wild

peat moors of Kinder Scout and the start of the Pennine Way which stretches 256 miles (412km) to the Scottish border. Walkers must be well equipped to cope with sudden weather changes, but the stiff climb to Kinder Downfall waterfall is worth the effort for the spectacular views to the west.

This Chatsworth estate village was planned by Paxton for the 6th Duke of Devonshire, as the old village spoiled the view. President Kennedy's sister, who married into the ducal family, is buried in the churchyard of George Gilbert Scott's church, as is Paxton.

A village where limestone and gritstone meet, reflected in varied stone of 17th and 18th-century houses. To the north of this former lead-mining centre, on Harthill Moor, is Robin Hood's Stride, a curious outcrop of gritstone which is popular with climbers.

EDENSOR
DERBYSHIRE. VILLAGE OFF B6012, 2 MILES (3KM) E OF BAKEWELL

ELTON
DERBYSHIRE. VILLAGE OFF B5056, 5 MILES (8KM) W OF MATLOCK

EYAM

DERBYSHIRE. VILLAGE OFF A623, 5 MILES (8KM) N OF BAKEWELL

It was in one of the houses near the church, known as Plague Cottages, that in September 1665 the village tailor took delivery of a box of clothes from London that was contaminated with plague germs. The deadly disease spread rapidly through the village, the people panicked and prepared to leave. But their parson, William Mompesson, encouraged them to stay, bravely isolating the place from the outside world in order to prevent the disease spreading across the county. The heroic villagers paid dearly for their courage, for out of some 350 inhabitants, 259 died. Whole families were wiped out; the graves of one entire family, the Rileys, can be seen to the west of the village. Mompesson closed the church and held services in the open air in Cucklett Delph. His wife was one of the victims and her grave may be seen in the churchyard.

Despite reminders of its sad past, Eyam (pronounced 'Eem') is none

the less one of the Peak District's most pleasing villages. It has a good variety of houses built solidly, in the 17th and 18th centuries, in local gritstone and in traditional Peakland styles. Some border the square, others line the sloping main street. Beside the church is a Saxon cross, its cross-head, unusually, still intact. The ancient tradition of well-dressing is practised here.

A beautiful 17th-century manor house built and still occupied by the Wright family. It is a cosy and intimate house with a stone-flagged hall, Jacobean staircase and an old kitchen. Numerous items of furniture, portraits, tapestries and objects of interest, accumulated over the centuries, are on display. A craft centre is housed in the former farmyard.

Open late Mar–early Nov, certain days.

Eyam Hall
(W OF CHURCH)
TEL: 01433 631976

Eyam churchyard has many graves of plague victims

FENNY BENTLEY
*DERBYSHIRE. VILLAGE ON
A515, 2 MILES (3KM)
N OF ASHBOURNE*

A southern Peak District village, with a medieval hall, now part of a farm. It lies near the Tissington Trail, a cycling and walking route on a former railway line.

(See also Cycle ride: The Tissington Trail, page 78.)

FLASH
*STAFFORDSHIRE. VILLAGE OFF
A53, 4 MILES (6.5KM)
SW OF BUXTON*

Claimed as the highest village in England and close to the source of the River Dove, Flash stands on an exposed moorland landscape enjoyed by walkers.

GLOSSOP
*DERBYSHIRE. TOWN ON A57,
13 MILES (21KM) E OF
MANCHESTER*

This northern Peak District town at the foot of Snake Pass has as a backdrop the spectacular moorland scenery of Bleaklow. Glossop was designed with formal squares and public buildings for the Duke of Norfolk in the 1820s and 30s, and the town flourished with the growth of the cotton mills. The site of *Melandra* Roman fort is on the edge of a modern housing estate. Old Glossop, a village uphill to the east, has narrow streets and lovely houses dating mainly from the 17th century. Numerous special events held here include a lively Victorian weekend in early September.

THE GOYT VALLEY
*DERBYSHIRE. VALLEY ON
WESTERN EDGE OF THE PEAK
DISTRICT*

The River Goyt rises on the wild and windswept moors and flows north near the Derbyshire–Cheshire border through the Errwood and Fernilee reservoirs, where there are car parks and woodland walks. Errwood car park, near the ruins of Errwood Hall, is the usual starting point for visitors to the valley.

GRINDLEFORD
*DERBYSHIRE. VILLAGE ON
B6001, 3 MILES (5KM)
S OF HATHERSAGE*

A small village in the valley of the River Derwent. Grindleford Station on the Hope Valley line is actually in Upper Padley, just to the north. An annual pilgrimage to Padley Chapel commemorates two Catholic martyrs of 1588.

GRINDON
*STAFFORDSHIRE. VILLAGE OFF
A523, 8 MILES (13KM)
NW OF ASHBOURNE*

There is a memorial in the church to the RAF crew who crashed while delivering supplies when this exposed moorland village was snowbound in 1947.

Romantic, battlemented Haddon Hall is like a house trapped in time; it has hardly changed for 400 years. It was started in the 12th century; then in the 18th century it was left to lie fallow by its owners, who were Earls and then Dukes of Rutland. They lived at Belvoir Castle instead, leaving Haddon Hall as perhaps the most perfect example of a medieval manor house in England. The oldest part is the painted chapel; the kitchen and the banqueting hall with its minstrels' gallery are of the 14th century; and there is a later long gallery leading to beautiful terraced rose gardens. Dorothy Vernon, a daughter of the house, is said to have eloped from here with John Manners in 1567. The steps and bridge linked with the elopement were not built until the 17th century – but the marriage of Dorothy and John certainly took place, so perhaps the story is true.

Open Etr–Sep, daily.

HADDON HALL
*DERBYSHIRE. 1½ MILES (2.5KM)
S OF BAKEWELL OFF A6
TEL: 01629 812855*

The Gardener's Cottage garden at Haddon Hall features some amusing topiary

HARTINGTON

DERBYSHIRE. VILLAGE ON B5054, 9 MILES (14.5KM) N OF ASHBOURNE

Stone cottages and an 1836 market hall surround the former market place and pond of this charming village beside the River Dove, forming the Staffordshire border. Higher up are a large medieval church and Hartington Hall (1611), now a youth hostel. Uniquely in Derbyshire, the cheese factory specialises in Stilton, producing this 'king of cheeses' far from the Vale of Belvoir dairies.

(See also Cycle ride: The Tissington Trail from Ashbourne to Hartington, page 78.)

HATHERSAGE

DERBYSHIRE. VILLAGE ON A625, 8 MILES (13KM) N OF BAKEWELL

Surprise View, Hathersage

This large, lively village is surrounded by moorland and gritstone edges, popular with walkers arriving by road from 'Surprise View' or by the Hope Valley train. The grave of Little John, Robin Hood's lieutenant and perhaps a Hathersage nail-maker, is in the churchyard. Eyre family monuments supplied the heroine's name, and the area became Morton in *Jane Eyre*, after Charlotte Brontë visited in 1845.

Huddled below the exposed moorland of Kinder Scout, the town grew up around wool-weaving and calico-printing works. This is a popular centre for hillwalkers, with the Sett Valley Trail for gentler walking and for riding alongside the river, which rushes down from the plateau to join the River Goyt at New Mills. Flooding was a frequent problem, causing the church to be rebuilt in 1818.

On 24 April 1932 Hayfield was the start of the well-publicised 'mass trespass' of about 500 ramblers on to Kinder Scout, a peaceful protest to gain free access to the moors and 'the right to roam'. When the ramblers encountered groups of gamekeepers on Sandy Heys, scuffles broke out, six ramblers were arrested and five were duly sentenced for up to six months in goal.

A tiny stone-built hamlet beside the River Dove amid splendid limestone scenery. There is a curious church of 1840 with an attached house under the same roof.

A picturesque village with relics of its textile past. Holme Moss is an area of Special Scientific Interest, noted for the tall TV transmitter mast which stands upon it.

A small mill town where picturesque groupings of sturdy gritstone cottages, ginnels, and courtyards mix with magnificent textile mills set proudly upon the landscape. Holmfirth is now synonymous with the television series *Last of the Summer Wine*, which was filmed here. There is a permanent photographic exhibition of the series.

Britain's first postcard museum, exhibiting a selection of Bamforth & Co sentimental and comic postcards and lantern slides. There are also video presentations of Bamforth's pioneering silent films and the dramatic story of the Holmfirth flood of 1852. Two other great floods took place here in 1777 and 1944.

Open all year, daily. Closed 21-26 Dec & 1 Jan.

The village gave its name to the Hope Valley at the confluence of the River Noe and Peakshole Water. Well-dressing takes place in June and early July and there are sheepdog trials, a weekly market and an agricultural show in late August. The railway station, across the Noe to the east of the village, is the starting point for a walk up Win Hill, a fine viewpoint. Lose Hill, another viewpoint is situated due west on the opposite side of the Noe.

HAYFIELD
Derbyshire. Small town on A624, 4 miles (6km) S of Glossop

HOLLINSCLOUGH
Staffordshire. Hamlet off B5053, 2 miles (3km) NW of Longnor

HOLME
West Yorkshire. Village on A6024, 3 miles (5km) SW of Holmfirth

HOLMFIRTH
West Yorkshire. Town on A635, 5 miles (8km) S of Huddersfield

Holmfirth Postcard Museum
47 Huddersfield Rd Tel: 01484 682231

HOPE
Derbyshire. Village on A625, 4 miles (6.5km) NW of Hathersage

ILAM

*STAFFORDSHIRE. VILLAGE OFF
A515, 4 MILES (6KM)
NW OF ASHBOURNE*

The village, with its attractive estate cottages and ancient church, is the starting point for walks through a beautiful stretch of the Manifold Valley. In summer the River Manifold disappears underground north of Ilam and reappears below Ilam Hall (a youth hostel). The river runs through wooded Ilam Park.

(See also Cycle ride: The Manifold Track and Ilam, page 56.)

LANGSETT

*SOUTH YORKSHIRE. VILLAGE AND
RESERVOIR ON A616 IN THE
NORTH-EAST CORNER OF THE
PEAK DISTRICT*

The small gritstone village (its name means 'long slope') is dominated by its reservoir, completed in 1904 and noted for its mock-Gothic valve tower styled on the gateway of Lancaster Castle. Langsett Barn bears a datestone of 1621 and is open during the season as a National Park Information Centre. From the car park there are walks along the shoreline of the reservoir through the woods and up onto the moors.

One of several rivers in the White Peak limestone area of the Peak District which disappears underground for parts of its course in summer, the River Lathkill rises in winter in a cave near Monyash. In dry periods, it emerges lower down near Over Haddon. Downstream, the lovely road-free ash and elm wooded dale was designated a National Nature Reserve in 1972.

    (See also Cycle ride: Ashford in the Water, page 6.)

A notable feature of the village is Lea Gardens, which extend through 3½ acres (1.5ha) of attractive woodland and are planted with rhododendrons, azaleas and rock plants; the gardens are open to the public.

    The activity centre at Lea Green was the former home of John Smedley, whose famous knitwear factory is near by.

LATHKILL DALE

DERBYSHIRE. BEAUTY SPOT; VALLEY OF RIVER LATHKILL E OF MONYASH

LEA

DERBYSHIRE. VILLAGE OFF A615, 3 MILES (5KM) SE OF MATLOCK

LEEK

*STAFFORDSHIRE. TOWN ON
A53, 10 MILES (16KM) NE OF
STOKE-ON-TRENT*

The 'capital' of the Staffordshire moorlands, Leek was once famous for silk weaving. A stroll around its busy streets reveals the Roebuck Inn (1627), Ash Almshouses (1676), weavers' cottages, the Nicholson Institute (art gallery) and former silk mills. Restored Brindley Mill houses displays relating to canal-builder James Brindley. St Edward's and All Saints' churches feature outstanding work by Victorian architects G E Street and Norman Shaw.

South-east of Leek is the Coombs Valley RSPB reserve, a lovely woodland area with a nature trail, walks and an information point.

LITTLE MORETON HALL

*CHESHIRE. 4 MILES (6.5KM)
SW OF CONGLETON
TEL: 01260 272018*

Little Moreton Hall is one of the most famous and best-preserved half-timbered houses in the country. Built within a moat and around a delightful cobbled courtyard, its exterior is a riot of black-and-white patterns, each square panel containing a rich variety of designs. The windows, too, are intricately glazed, again with various patterns picked out by the strips of lead. The Hall was begun in the middle of the 15th century for the Moreton family, powerful local landlords and tax collectors for the king, and further extensions were added up to 1580. The family continued to live there, except for a break of about 200 years when it was let out to tenants, until it was finally donated to the National Trust in 1937.

The east wing and the great hall, once the focus of day-to-day life on the estate, are the oldest parts of the house. Three items of furniture here are original to the house – the long refectory table, the 'great rounde table' which occupies the bay window and the 'cubborde of boxes'. Apart from these items, the rooms in the Hall are largely empty. No doubt authentic pieces with which to refurnish the house are not easy to come by, and the lack of them only serves to emphasise the wonderful architecture and proportions of each room.

The withdrawing room was the place to which the lord of the manor, his family and guests could retreat from the noise of the great hall and enjoy some privacy from the servants. Here the enormous roof timbers are moulded, and there is a magnificent overmantel carved with the royal arms of Elizabeth I.

When the house was extended in the 16th century the chapel was built, although the stained glass was not added until 1932. The panels of text are taken from the 1539 edition of the Tyndale Bible.

The upper storey of the south wing of the house is occupied by the superb long gallery, which stretches for 68ft (20m) beneath massive arch-braced roof trusses. The gallery would always have been relatively free of furniture, for its main purpose was for daily exercise and games – and a 17th-century tennis ball was found behind one of the panels.

Within the moated area of the house a formal knot garden can be found, charmingly designed to reproduce as closely as possible the style typical of the 17th century.

Open from late Mar–Oct, on selected afternoons.

The crazy angles and black-and-white façade of Little Moreton Hall

LITTON

*DERBYSHIRE. VILLAGE OFF
A623, 10 MILES (16KM)
NE OF BUXTON*

A pretty, compact village with 18th-century cottages and a green with a set of stocks close to the Red Lion pub. Many of the buildings have date-stones (the oldest is 1639).

LONGDENDALE

*GREATER MANCHESTER. VALLEY
OF THE RIVER ETHEROW,
TRIBUTARY OF THE GOYT*

This valley once marked the northern boundary of the Royal Forest of the Peak. Five reservoirs – Woodhead, Torside, Rhodeswater, Valehouse and Bottoms – were built by the Manchester Corporation in the 19th century to supply water to the growing city. At the time, they formed the largest man-made stretch of water in the world.

LONGNOR

*STAFFORDSHIRE. SMALL TOWN
ON B5053, 6 MILES (9.5KM)
SE OF BUXTON*

The small grey town between the rivers Manifold and Dove is surrounded by moorland. St Bartholomew's is a classical church of 1780 with a Venetian east window, but it preserves a carved Norman font from its predecessor. The town's old character survives in the cobbled Chapel Street, and a craft centre now occupies the market hall of 1873, built when Longnor was a wealthy farming community. Agricultural depression resulted in a declining population. When Longnor became a conservation area in 1977, new life was breathed into the village.

*The small town of Longnor
with its smithy*

The Longshaw Country Park and visitor centre (National Trust) has dramatic views and moorland walks. The estate's quarries produced millstones, some of which can still be seen, and grindstones for Sheffield's cutlery industry. The network of paths lead to the 'plague village' of Eyam and the ancient oak woodland of Padley Gorge. Three-day sheepdog trials are held in early September.

Home of the Legh family for 600 years and the largest house in Cheshire, Lyme Park is now in the care of the National Trust. Part of the original Elizabethan house remains with 18th- and 19th-century additions by Giacomo Leoni and Lewis Wyatt. Four centuries of period interiors include Mortlake tapestries, Grinling Gibbons carvings, and a unique collection of English clocks. The house is set in extensive historic gardens with a conservatory by Wyatt, a lake, and the 'Dutch' garden. There is a 1,400-acre (566-ha) park, home to red and fallow deer, with magnificent views of the Pennines and the Cheshire Plain. Details of special events are available on request.

Open: Hall, late Mar–Oct, most afternoons, tel: 01663 766492 for details. Park open all year. Gardens Apr–Oct, daily; telephone for winter opening.

LONGSHAW ESTATE
Derbyshire. Scenic area off A625, 7 miles (11km) SW of Sheffield

LYME PARK
Cheshire. Disley, off A6
Tel: 01663 762023

*J*ust off the A537 between Macclesfield and Buxton, Tegg's Nose Country Park is on the site of a former quarry on the south-western edge of the Pennines. It affords spectacular views across the Cheshire Plain, and makes a good starting point for several invigorating walks.

(400-m) summit (viewing plaque provided) are justly famous, extending west across the Cheshire Plain, and east over Macclesfield Forest to the heights of the western Peak District.

HOW TO GET THERE

Take the A537 to Buxton from Macclesfield, turning right as you climb out of the town on to a minor road signposted for the park. Coming from Buxton, turn left by the chapel at Walker Barn on to Cat and Fiddle Road; the park is well signposted.

FACILITIES

Visitor centre and toilets, including for disabled people.
Refreshments kiosk (open on summer weekends).
Picnic tables in sheltered spots.
Guided walks available during the summer.
Toposcope for views.

Most of the pinkish gritstone which paves the streets of the silk town of Macclesfield came from Tegg's Nose Quarry, high above the town on the edge of the Pennines. Cheshire County Council converted the area into a 133-acre (54ha) country park when the quarry closed in 1955.

The picnic area, visitor centre and toilets are by the roadside at Windy Way.

    The views from the 1,300-ft

The picnic site at Tegg's Nose Country Park

Picnic site

What to do

There are three waymarked trails around the peak, lasting from half an hour to half a day, and the adventurous can take an orienteering course. Tegg's Nose also links up with the 18-mile (29km) Gritstone Trail, which runs from Lyme Park to Rushton Spencer. In winter, Tegg's Nose is a favourite spot for sledging. There is some climbing and abseiling for the experts on the main quarry face.

In Tegg's Nose Wood, by the reservoir to the south, oak, mountain ash and holly flourish, together with ferns, mosses and an abundant bird life including spotted flycatchers in summer.

Close by

Macclesfield owes its fame to the silk-weaving mills which grew up here in the 18th and 19th centuries. There are two museums, the Silk Museum in the Heritage Centre on Roe Street, and the Paradise Mill Working Silk Museum on Park Lane, which tell

Ridgegate Reservoir, Macclesfield Forest

the fascinating story of how silk came to the Bollin Valley. Three miles (5km) south-west, near Congleton, is Gawsworth Hall, a late 15th-century manor house still in private hands (see also page 57); and the spa town of Buxton, with its fine Georgian architecture and show cave of Poole's Cavern, is 12 miles (19km) away on the A537 (see also pages 17 and 52).

MACCLESFIELD

CHESHIRE. TOWN ON A52
(A523), 10 MILES (16KM)
S OF STOCKPORT

Although its origins lie in medieval times, Macclesfield really grew up around the textile industry and retains the look of an early mill town with terraced weavers' cottages, mills, Georgian town houses and Nonconformist churches, in the foothills of the Peak District. It became established as the country's silk-weaving centre, and the silk history of the town now attracts many visitors. Paradise Mill was the last hand-loom weaving business to operate in the town, finally closing for production in 1981. It reopened in 1984 as part of the Macclesfield Silk Museum.

The medieval core of the town, embracing the church, the town hall and the market place, is still very much the focal point, at the junction of Chestergate and Mill Street, both of which are busy, pleasant shopping streets.

(See also Picnic site: Tegg's Nose Country Park, page 50.)

Gawsworth Hall

2½ MILES (4KM) S OF
MACCLESFIELD OFF A536
TEL: 01260 223456

A fine example of Cheshire black-and-white architecture, Gawsworth Hall was built in the second half of the 15th century and for many years was the home of the Fitton family. Today it is a peaceful and serene household, giving little hint of its eventful past.

They were known as the 'Fighting Fittons' in those days, and Mary

Farm buildings in Macclesfield

Fitton, 'the wayward maid of Gawsworth', is said to be the 'Dark Lady' of Shakespeare's sonnets. The last professional jester in England, Maggoty Johnson, lived at Gawsworth where he was dancing master to the children, and is buried near by in 'Maggoty Johnson's Wood'.

Originally the house was built around a quadrangle, but it was reduced in size by Charles Gerard, 2nd Earl of Macclesfield, at about the end of the 17th century. Today it has all the charm and character of a medieval house, with fine old timbers and ornate fireplaces, and is filled with comfortable old furniture, paintings, sculpture and armour. The delightful little chapel has beautiful stained glass by Burne-Jones and William Morris, while out in the lovely grounds is a rare survivor – an Elizabethan tilting ground.

Open mid Mar–early Oct, every afternoon.

Owned by the National Trust, the beautiful parkland at Hare Hill also features a pretty walled garden and pergola. A brilliant display of rhododendrons and azaleas can be seen in late spring.

Open late Mar–late Oct, certain days. Parties by written appointment with the Head Gardener. Special openings (to see rhododendrons and azaleas) mid May–early Jun, daily.

Hare Hill
4 MILES (6.5KM) N OFF
B5087
TEL: 01625 828981

Macclesfield Silk Museum
HERITAGE CENTRE, ROE ST
TEL: 01625 613210

The silk museum presents the story of silk in Macclesfield through a colourful audio-visual programme, exhibitions, textiles, garments, models and room settings. It is situated in the Heritage Centre, formerly a Sunday school for child labourers. A full programme of musical and artistic events is available throughout the year at the Heritage Centre.

Open all year, daily. Closed Good Fri, 24–26 Dec & 1 Jan.

Paradise Mill
PARK LANE
TEL: 01625 618228

An award-winning museum where knowledgeable guides, many of them former silk mill workers, illustrate the silk production process with the help of demonstrations from weavers. The museum was a working silk mill until 1981 when the last handloom weaver retired, and 26 handlooms have been fully restored in their original setting. Exhibitions and room settings give an impression of working conditions at the mill during the 1930s.

Open all year, most afternoons. Closed Good Fri, 24–26 Dec & 1 Jan.

West Park Museum
WEST PARK, PRESTBURY RD
TEL: 01625 619831

A small but significant collection of Egyptian antiquities can be seen at this museum, together with a wide range of fine and decorative arts. The paintings on display are from the 19th and early 20th centuries and include the work of the bird artist, Charles Tunnicliffe. Items relating to local history are also shown. The museum was established in 1898 by the Brocklehurst family, and is on the edge of one of the earliest parks founded by voluntary subscriptions.

Open Etr–Dec, most afternoons. Closed Good Fri, 25–26 Dec & 1 Jan.

gazetteer

The river rises on the northern edge of Staffordshire and runs south through moorland to join the River Dove near Thorpe. At Ecton, it starts to flow beneath dramatic hills, and there are caves in steep valley sides near Wetton, notably the huge Thor's Cave. Prehistoric sites abound on both sides of the river. The most popular riverside destination for visitors is Ilam.

MANIFOLD, RIVER
STAFFORDSHIRE. RIVER, TRIBUTARY OF THE RIVER DOVE

The Manifold Valley, viewed from Thor's Cave

The first 8 miles (13km), from Hulme End to Waterhouses, are along the popular Manifold Track, one of the best 'off-highway' cycling routes in the country. It is surfaced throughout, and only a short section between Swainsley and Wettonmill is shared with light traffic. Riders wanting a really easy day might return along the trail from Waterhouses to Hulme End. Beyond Waterhouses, the main route climbs to open country before descending to Ilam, one of Staffordshire's loveliest villages. The return ride offers a diversion to visit Milldale at the head of Dovedale.

INFORMATION

Distance
20 miles (32km),
with 8 miles (13km) off-road

Difficulty
Moderate

OS Map
Landranger 1:50,000 sheet 119
(Buxton, Matlock & Dovedale)

Tourist Information
Buxton. tel: 01298 25106

Cycle Shops/Hire
Brown End Farm, Waterhouses,
tel: 01538 308313;
Peak National Park Cycle Hire,
Waterhouses, tel: 01538
308609;
Parsley Hay Cycle Hire (Tissington
Trail). Tel: 01298 84493

Nearest Railway Station
Buxton (10 miles/16km)

Refreshments
The Manifold Valley Hotel at
Hulme End serves pub meals, and
children are welcome at The
George; tea rooms at Wettonmill
and Lea Farm; café at Ilam Hall;
tea rooms in Alstonefield.

START
Hulme End lies in the south-west
corner of the Peak District
National Park, on the B5054,

*Cyclists on the Manifold Track at
Hulme End*

Cycle ride

2 miles (3km) west of Hartington between Buxton and Ashbourne. Park in the car park at the start of The Manifold Track (honesty box for payment).

DIRECTIONS

1. From the back of the car park, turn on to the Manifold Track cycle route, heading south. In

1 mile (1.5km) at Ecton cross over the byroad (gates) and continue along the trail with Ecton Hill on the left. At Swainsley the route passes through a well-lit tunnel. From here the trail is also used by light motor traffic, so care is required. Continue along the route to reach Wettonmill.

Beeston Tor, near Weag's Bridge

2. At Wettonmill there is a choice of ways: either continue on the trail, or fork right through a ford on the 'old' road. The routes re-join in ½ mile (1km) at Redhurst Crossing – turn through the gate here and continue along the trail following the windings of the River

The Manifold Valley Hotel at Hulme End is a popular spot for refreshments

Manifold. Continue to reach a junction at Weag's Bridge. A steep road on the right leads to the pretty village of Grindon. Cross over the lane, pass through a gate and continue along the Manifold Track. This soon leaves the River Manifold and turns instead along the valley of its tributary, the River Hamps. Stay on the trail along the valley, passing woodland on the steep flank of Soles Hill to the left. Continue, and near a disused quarry, come out at the A523 near Waterhouses.

3. Turn left with care on to the busy A523 towards Ashbourne. Climb for ½ mile (1km) and take the first turning left on to a byroad. On the outskirts of Calton village turn left, and turn left again in ½ mile (1km), heading north. Climb into open country and descend, to reach Throwley Hall in 2 miles (3km). Pass through the gates and yard of Throwley Hall, then continue along the lane. Descend and bear left to cross a bridge over the River Manifold. Climb to a T-junction with Ilam Country Park on the right. Turn right and descend into Ilam.

4. From Ilam you can stay on this road and turn left by the Izaak Walton Hotel to explore the foot of scenic Dovedale.

Otherwise, retrace the route back through Ilam and keep right at the junction towards Hopedale and Alstonefield. Climb steeply for 1 mile (1.5km) then continue into open country. Keep left at Stanshope, and descend to a T-junction. Turn right here, and descend into Hopedale.

5. For a hilly but scenic diversion to the route here, turn almost immediately right, past the inn, and continue to Milldale. Bear left in Milldale beside the River Dove, and at Lode Mill turn sharply left and climb steeply into Alstonefield. Turn right at the village green towards Hulme End, to rejoin the main route which joins this road from Wetton.

To continue on the main route go back through Hopedale and turn right, and then shortly bear left towards Wetton. Keep left and then turn right to explore the village. Leave Wetton, heading north-east towards Hulme East, passing prehistoric burial sites on Wetton Hill to the left. At the junction, turn left, and in 2 miles (3km) reach the B5054 at Hulme End. Turn left, and left again to

A cottage garden at Ilam

Cycle ride

return to the car park.

PLACES OF INTEREST

Hulme End

The car park is the original site of the terminus station and engine sheds of the Manifold Valley Light Railway, which was closed in 1934. It was constructed to carry milk from the surrounding farms but also operated a passenger service.

Wettonmill

This beautiful spot is well worth a pause, if only to explore the caves in the hillside opposite. There is also a small tea room, toilets, and a camp site. The River Manifold disappears underground here into 'swallets' and, except after heavy rainfall, does not reappear until it reaches Ilam.

Weag's Bridge

A picturesque stone bridge crosses the river here, below the

WHAT TO LOOK OUT FOR

The pale-coloured, porous limestone rock found in this area of the Peak District has given it the name of the 'White Peak'; if you look carefully at boulders in the drystone walls you may see signs of fossilised plants and animals.

---

lofty heights of Beeston Tor. A steep road leads up to the village of Grindon; in the church there is a memorial to an RAF crew killed when their plane crashed while dropping food supplies when the village was cut off by snow.

Ilam

Ilam is one of the most beautiful villages in Staffordshire, with an unusually tall Gothic cross and a pleasing bridge over the River Manifold, which reappears here after flowing underground from Wettonmill. Ilam is a model village, largely rebuilt during the 19th century. Its attractive country park is in the care of the National Trust, and the Old Hall is a popular youth hostel. This is also the gateway to the beautiful Dovedale area.

(See also page 44.)

Wetton

This pleasing old village of stone cottages is a good centre for exploring this part of the Peak District. A ½-mile (1-km) walk leads to the dramatic Thor's Cave, a vast cavern overlooking the Manifold Valley (see page 87); the cave was once inhabited.

(See also page 83.)

Wettonmill on the River Manifold

Go back in time to the days when narrow boats were 'legged' through tunnels under the Pennines, and when later on, railway engineers faced the enormous problem presented by this great natural barrier. In an old tunnel-keeper's cottage, in a surprisingly rural backwater at Tunnel End, the story is skilfully explained to visitors.

HOW TO GET THERE

From the centre of Marsden, on the A62 Huddersfield–Oldham road, take the minor road past the church which ascends towards the railway station, crossing the canal and the River Colne. Above the railway and the river, turn left on to Reddisher Road; Tunnel End is signposted to the left after about ½ mile (1km).

There are only about 20 car park spaces at Tunnel End, so

Why not take a trip? Tunnel End, Marsden

another interesting and enjoyable way to reach it is by narrow boat from Marsden, where a shuttle service runs most weekends.

FACILITIES

Tunnel End Canal and Countryside Centre.
Education and audio-visual rooms and shop.
Refreshments available.
Toilets provided.
Start of Standedge Trail at Marsden.

DIRECTIONS

Four tunnels emerge from under the formidable barrier of the Pennines at Tunnel End, Marsden. The tunnel which takes the Huddersfield Narrow Canal under the bleak moorlands of Standedge took navvies over 16 years to build and opened in 1811; measuring 4¼ miles (7km), it is still the longest canal tunnel in the country. Narrow boats were

originally 'legged' through the tunnel by boatmen lying on their backs and pushing against the walls with their feet. Of the three railway tunnels, the first, completed in 1849, was single-track; the London and North Western Railway tunnel followed in 1871; and the third, a double-track tunnel still in use as part of the main trans-Pennine route, was completed in 1894.

All these stories and something of the abundant natural history of the area are told in the imaginative Tunnel End Canal and Countryside Centre, housed in the former tunnel keeper's cottage where the canal disappears into the hillside.

A stroll up behind the cottage along Ainsley Lane passes the silted up remains of the Tunnel End Reservoir, built to feed the canal in 1798. Known locally as Boat Lane, Ainsley Lane was the first part of the journey over the

The River Holme and the 'Wrinkled Stocking', Holmfirth

hills taken by the horses while the boat was being 'legged' through the tunnel. The lane also passes the site where the navvies lived in a temporary camp while the tunnels were being built.

CLOSE BY

The Standedge Trail (12 miles/ 19km long) starts from Marsden, using old turnpike roads and tracks to cross the moors to Diggle. Many features of historical and archaeological interest are passed on this route, but it should only be attempted by well-equipped walkers.

Marsden is on the edge of *Last of the Summer Wine* country, centred on Holmfirth about 10 miles (16km) away. Children of all ages will enjoy Holmfirth's Postcard Museum.

(See also page 43.)

MARSDEN

WEST YORKSHIRE. TOWN ON A62, 7 MILES (11KM) SW OF HUDDERSFIELD

The centre of this textile town is a conservation area. On Marsden Moor (National Trust) there is evidence of historic packhorse routes.

(See also Picnic Site: Tunnel End Visitor Centre, Marsden, page 60.)

MATLOCK

DERBYSHIRE. TOWN ON A6, 9 MILES (14.5KM) SW OF CHESTERFIELD

Matlock is a popular Derbyshire Dales town and tourist centre, bordering the Peak National Park. Peak Rail steam trains provide an enjoyable ride to Northwood from Matlock Riverside. The County Council offices occupy Smedley's grand 1852 hydropathic hotel, which once attracted crowds to rest, recuperate and enjoy views of Riber Castle, now a fauna reserve and wildlife park, perched on the opposite hilltop.

From Hall Leys Park's attractive gardens and recreation facilities, the River Derwent flows on through a deep limestone gorge, shared by both railway and A6, to Matlock Bath's wooded walks and autumn illuminations. A cable car spanning the gorge gives easy access to the Heights of Abraham pleasure grounds. High Tor precipice, on the opposite hillside, offers both a challenge to rock-climbers, and gentler footpaths to the summit.

Heights of Abraham
ON A6
TEL: 01629 582365

High on a hill above the village of Matlock Bath are the grounds of the Heights of Abraham. Until recently the climb to the summit was only for the very energetic, but now alpine-style cable cars provide a leisurely and spectacular way of reaching the top from their starting point near Matlock Bath Railway Station. Once inside the grounds there is plenty to do for the whole family. Two famous show caverns provide fascinating tours; one is introduced by a multivision programme and the other tells the story of a 17th-century lead miner. A coffee shop, licensed restaurant and picnic sites take advantage of the superb views. There is also a nature trail, the Victoria Prospect Tower and play area, the Owl Maze, the Explorers' Challenge and landscaped water garden. Your cable car ticket

The Heights of Abraham can be reached by cable car

includes all the attractions in the grounds and both cavern tours.

Open daily Etr–Oct; for autumn & winter opening, please telephone for details.

A large and rewarding display, ideal for families, explains the history of the Derbyshire lead industry from Roman times to the present day. The geology of the area, mining and smelting processes, the quarrying and the people who worked in the industry, are all illustrated by a series of static and moving exhibits and an audio-visual display. The museum also features an early 19th-century water pressure pumping engine – the only one of its kind in Britain. A new exhibit is the interactive 'Hazards of Mining' display.

Open all year, daily. Closed 25 Dec.

Currently being restored to recreate an authentic feel of the 1920s and 1930s, these old lead and fluorspar workings make interesting viewing. A self-guided tour illustrates the geology, mineralisation and mining techniques.

Open all year. Closed 25 Dec.

Peak District Mining Museum
THE PAVILION
(OFF A6)
TEL: *01629 583834*

Temple Mine
TEMPLE RD
(OFF A6)
TEL: *01629 583834*

MIDDLETON

DERBYSHIRE. VILLAGE ON B5023, 1 MILE (1.5KM) N OF WIRKSWORTH

A limestone-quarrying village. Middleton Top beam-engine, steamed regularly in summer, was once used to haul wagons up Middleton Incline on the Cromford and High Peak Railway. There is a visitor centre and cycle hire along High Peak Trail.

MILLER'S DALE

DERBYSHIRE. VILLAGE ON B6049, 5 MILES (8KM) E OF BUXTON

The village takes its name from one of the best known of several lovely limestone dales along the River Wye. It grew in the 1860s to provide housing for the rail men and the quarry workers and their families, but today all that remains are some old houses, former textile mills, and lime kilns dating from 1878. The viaduct now carries the Monsal Trail leisure route on the dismantled railway track along the length of the valley.

MONSAL DALE

DERBYSHIRE. BEAUTY SPOT OFF A6, E OF TADDINGTON

A beautiful limestone dale, through which the River Wye flows, with fine views from Monsal Head. The dramatic 1860s viaduct now forms part of the Monsal Trail.

NEW MILLS

DERBYSHIRE. TOWN OFF A6, 8 MILES (13KM) NW OF BUXTON

New Mills takes its name from Tudor cornmills, but the town grew largely through the development of 18th- and 19th-century cotton mills. The textile industry was later joined by engineering industries and the confectionery trade. The Sett Valley Trail provides an attractive walk or cycle ride from Hayfield alongside a tributary of the River Goyt.

ONECOTE

STAFFORDSHIRE. VILLAGE ON B5053, 4 MILES (6.5KM) E OF LEEK

The Jervis Arms beside the River Hamps is a welcome feature of this scattered village in high moorland country. The 18th-century Church of St Luke has an unusual, Venetian east window.

The village is in limestone country overlooking Lathkill Dale. It was formerly a lead-mining area, and a target for the 1850s 'gold rush', when iron pyrites (fool's gold) was found.

(See also Cycle ride: Ashford in the Water, page 6.)

A village with stone houses and an 1870s church set around a green. Brick-built Parwich Hall, standing on a hillside, was completed in 1747. The Roystone Grange Archeology Trail runs near by. There are over 70 mysterious embanked Bronze Age circles on the moor.

Peaceful Monsal Dale

OVER HADDON
DERBYSHIRE. VILLAGE OFF B5055, 2 MILES (3KM) SW OF BAKEWELL

PARWICH
DERBYSHIRE. VILLAGE OFF A515, 5 MILES (8KM) N OF ASHBOURNE

THE PEAK DISTRICT NATIONAL PARK

There are really two distinct Peak Districts – two areas of equally beautiful but totally different landscapes, each of which has its own avid supporters. Kinder Scout and the northern moors of Bleaklow and Black Hill, whose very names give away their hard, masculine nature, form the biggest block of what is known as the Dark Peak. The Dark Peak spreads around the northern, western and eastern sides of the National Park like a horseshoe, while the softer, more

The Sheepwash Bridge at Ashford in the Water

feminine landscape of the White Peak occupies the centre and the south. It is a distinction based on the underlying geology of the area, for the Dark Peak moors, tors and edges (escarpments) are formed by sombre-coloured millstone grit, and the White Peak plateau and dales from pearly-white limestone. Both rocks are sedimentary, laid down during the carboniferous period about 350 million years ago when the land we now know as Britain was much closer to the equator.

The limestone is the fossilised remains of countless millions of tiny sea creatures and organisms which were laid down in a shallow, semi-tropical sea. This was later overlaid with mud and grit deposited by a huge prehistoric river, forming the grits, shales and sandstones of the Dark Peak. Countless millions of years of erosion by wind, water and ice have gradually and remorselessly removed the gritstone cover from the centre and south of the Peak, revealing the dazzling white limestone skeleton beneath. This is all the stuff of textbook geology, making the Peak a popular place for students of that science.

However, you don't have to be a geologist to appreciate the land-scapes of Britain's first National Park. The 22 million day visits it receives every year show it to be one of the most popular National Parks not only in Britain, but the world, and the area it covers seems to have something for just about everybody. Visitors come to the Peak for many reasons, but for most it provides the chance to escape into beautiful, unspoilt countryside from the towns and cities of the north and Midlands. It is sometimes hard to believe as you look out across the wild moorland heights of Kinder or Bleaklow that just over a dozen miles (19km) in either direction, east or west, are the city centres of Manchester and Sheffield. This accessibility is at once one of the Peak's great attractions, and one of its greatest problems. The sheer number of those visitors can cause congestion in the small villages and narrow country roads, and erosion on a massive scale on some of the most popular footpaths, notably the Pennine Way which starts its 250 miles (400km) journey north at Edale.

The moors and dales of the Peak were not always as easily accessible as they are today. In the 1930s the highest and wildest moors of the Dark Peak, including Kinder and Bleaklow, were out of bounds to the rambler because they were strictly preserved grouse

Looking east on the ascent at Tintwistle

moors, watched over by patrolling gamekeepers. The 1932 'mass trespass' on Kinder Scout, after which five ramblers were imprisoned, saw the start of the end of that restriction and today, thanks to access agreements negotiated by the National Park with landowners, over 80 square miles (207sq km) have open access.

Yet bog trotting across the moors is not everyone's cup of tea and many people prefer the gentler walking available on the 1,600 miles (2,575km) of public rights of way in the National Park. Many of these are on the limestone plateau of the White Peak, where pretty stone-built villages like Bakewell, Tideswell, Hartington, Foolow and Monyash seem to grow almost organically from the landscape. Others pass through the spectacular, crag-rimmed limestone dales of the White Peak, home of the rarest and best of the Peak's wildlife, which have been famous as visitor attractions since the 17th century.

The best known of these dales is undoubtedly Dovedale, the praises of which were first extrolled by Izaak Walton and Charles Cotton in the anglers' bible, The Compleat Angler, first published in 1653. Walton dubbed the Dove 'the princess of rivers', and tourists have been agreeing with him ever since. But many other dales, such as Lathkill Dale (part of the Derbyshire Dales National Nature Reserve), Bradford Dale, near Youlgrave, and the Manifold valley, just over the border in Staffordshire, are equally beautiful and often not as crowded as Dovedale, especially in high summer.

The first real tourist guide to the Peak was written by Thomas Hobbes, philosopher and tutor to the Cavendish family at Chatsworth, whose De Mirabilibus Pecci, or The Wonders of the Peak, published in 1636, became the basis for a generally accepted 'grand tour' of the region. Charles Cotton of Hartington, co-author of The Compleat Angler, later rehashed Hobbes' seven 'wonders' in his

The hamlet of Pilsbury, in Dovedale

own version, published in 1681. Nearly all these wonders were in the White Peak, and included places like Peak Cavern, the largest cave entrance in Britain at Castleton, Poole's Cavern in Buxton, and Eldon Hole, a large open pothole near Peak Forest. Mam Tor was included because of its unstable east face which constantly sheds rocks and debris, earning it the nickname the 'Shivering Mountain', and another wonder was the palatial home of the Dukes of Devonshire at Chatsworth, newly won from the wilderness.

For many people coming from the south, the east or the Midlands, the introduction to the Peak and the Pennines is the White Peak, and the first thing that strikes these visitors from the lowland shires is the

intricate system of drystone walls which spreads across the green pastures like a net. It has been estimated that, in the White Peak alone, there are 26,000 miles (41,600km) of drystone walls which, if built around the equator, would more than encircle the earth. These are mostly a legacy from the Enclosure Movements of the 18th and 19th centuries, although some have recently been archaeologically dated to the Roman period. Certainly, early man found the Peak very much to his liking and the area is a rich treasure-house for the archaeologist and landscape historian. Almost every hilltop in this part of the Peak paradoxically carries the name 'low', which denotes a tumulus or burial mound, usually dating from the Bronze Age. Even earlier is the famous Neolithic stone circle, or henge, of Arbor Low, near Monyash, which has been dubbed 'the Stonehenge of the North'. But Arbor Low's stones, unlike those of its Wiltshire contemporary, lie recumbent within a grassy embankment which has a Bronze Age barrow on its rim.

Later in the Bronze Age there seems to have been a movement towards the apparently inhospitable moors of the Dark Peak and in places like the Eastern Moor, west of Chesterfield and Sheffield, entire self-contained communities of this period have been identified. The reason for this movement is thought to have been related to a change in the climate of Britain, and weather conditions were certainly more amenable. Today, the moors are only home to hawk and hare.

One of the largest and highest Iron Age hillforts in the Pennines is found at Mam Tor, at the head of the broad Hope Valley on the boundary between the White and Dark Peak. On this windswept, 1,695-ft (517-m) hill of shale and grit a sizeable population once lived, perhaps using their 'town in the sky' as a summertime shelter from which they could watch over their flocks of grazing animals. It is one of several hillforts which are scattered about the Dark Peak,

usually overlooking the broad river valleys which separate it from the lush pastures of the limestone country.

The Romans came to the Peak to exploit the easily accessible veins of lead ore which criss-cross the White Peak. Their lead-mining centre, which we know from surviving pigs (ingots) of lead was called Ludutarum, has still not been satisfactorily identified, and the only sizeable Roman settlement which has been excavated is the small fortlet of Navio at Brough a few miles from Mam Tor in the Hope Valley, which may have been built to defend those lead-mining interests. But the heyday of the lead-mining industry in the Peak was during the 18th century, when over 10,000 miners were at work in the White Peak area. The great landowners of the Peak, such as the Dukes of Devonshire at Chatsworth and the Dukes of Rutland from nearby Haddon Hall, gained much of their wealth from the mineral rights exploited by mining in the Peak, and they left a legacy of rolling parkland and beautiful stately homes which adorn the valleys of the Derwent and the Wye.

The Peak has always been a dynamic, working landscape, and wherever the visitor looks he will see evidence of man's hand. The huge limestone quarries, such as those which excluded Buxton and Matlock from the boundaries of the National Park, are still very visible features in the Park, and an important source of employment for the 38,000 residents.

Even in the apparently wildest places, such as the valley of the Upper Derwent in the shadow of Bleaklow, the landscape of lake and forest is the result of human activities. The triple reservoirs of Howden, Derwent and Ladybower were created to provide water for the growing industrial populations of the surrounding cities, and the trees were planted to protect water purity. Today, they are popular places for visitors and the subject of a traffic management scheme similar to one first introduced in the Goyt Valley on the western side of the Park. Other pioneering projects by the independent National Parks Authority have included the transformation of derelict railway lines, such as the Tissington and High Peak Trails, into pleasant walking and riding routes. So, despite the pressures, the Peak still provides the 'great escape' for the citizens of the surrounding cities.

Woodland at Win Hill

PEAK FOREST

Derbyshire. Hamlet on A623, 4 miles (6.5km) SE of Chapel-en-le-Frith

THE ROACHES

Staffordshire. Millstone grit outcrop, NE of Leek off the A53

The Roaches

Despite its name this is an almost treeless area, but it came under royal forest law, giving it scope as a venue for clandestine marriages until 1804. Near by is Eldon Hole, which is the largest open pothole in the Peak District.

Hen Cloud, Ramshaw Rocks and The Roaches are dramatic gritstone outcrops popular with rock-climbers. Ramshaw Rocks, an outlier of The Roaches, tower above the A53 displaying a feature like a face. A footpath follows the crest of The Roaches, linking it with Back Forest to the north and the natural chasm known as Lud's Church. The area was famous as the home of a colony of wallabies, but these are now gone.

The rivers Derwent and Wye meet at Rowsley, a Haddon Hall estate village of 17th- and 18th-century houses and a gateway to the National Park. Caudwell's Mill, a working 19th-century flour mill, is also a craft centre, and there is a path beside the mill race and along the banks of the River Wye.

This splendid Sheffield—Glossop moorland route is frequently closed by winter snow. It takes its name from the Snake Inn, built by the Duke of Devonshire soon after he built the road, and was named after his family's emblem.

One of the oldest cotton towns in the country which grew rapidly during the Industrial Revolution, Stalybridge retains a handsome Victorian appearance. The Astley Cheetham Art Gallery contains 14th- and 15th-century Florentine paintings.

The village is situated on a steep and winding road below Stanton Moor. The initials WPT, carved into the lintels of many doorways in the village, refer to William Paul Thornhill who built most of the village in the 1830s. His family lived at Stanton Hall. To the south, on Stanton Moor, are three prehistoric stone circles; the most famous is known as Nine Ladies, and just outside the circle stands the King's Stone. Numerous tumuli dot the moorland.

Stockport is a large market town originally built on a red sandstone cliff overlooking the River Mersey. The 700-year-old market place, adjacent to the Merseyway shopping precinct and built on massive stilts over the River Mersey, is surrounded by buildings of historic interest, including the Church of St Mary. The chancel dates from the 14th century but there is evidence of a church dating from 1150 on this site. The nave and the tower were rebuilt in 1813, following a partial collapse which was blamed on a marathon bell-ringing session to celebrate Nelson's victory at Trafalgar.

Stockport has thrived as a market town for hundreds of years, and during the Industrial Revolution was a notable centre for textile and hat manufacture. Stockport Museum records the history of hat-making in the town.

Other noteworthy buildings include Stockport's 'wedding cake' town hall, so called because of its white façade and high, tiered clock tower. The Tunnel Shelters, a maze of underground tunnels cut for use as air-raid shelters during World War II, are open to the public, and the famous illuminated Stockport Railway Viaduct with 27 arches, built in 1840, dominates the town.

ROWSLEY
DERBYSHIRE. VILLAGE ON A6, 3 MILES (5KM) SE OF BAKEWELL

SNAKE PASS
DERBYSHIRE. MOUNTAIN PASS ON A57, SE OF GLOSSOP

STALYBRIDGE
GREATER MANCHESTER. TOWN OFF A635, 8 MILES (13KM) E OF MANCHESTER

STANTON IN PEAK
DERBYSHIRE. VILLAGE OFF A6, 1 MILE (1.5KM) SW OF ROWSLEY

STOCKPORT
GREATER MANCHESTER. TOWN OFF M63, 6 MILES (9.5KM) SE OF MANCHESTER

STOCKSBRIDGE

SOUTH YORKSHIRE. TOWN OFF A6102, 8 MILES (13KM) NW OF SHEFFIELD

Stocksbridge is a self-contained, semi-rural community in the valley of the River Don and on the edge of Howden Moors, which grew around the still-dominant steelworks.

STONEY MIDDLETON

DERBYSHIRE. VILLAGE ON A623, 5 MILES (8KM) N OF BAKEWELL

A village in Middleton Dale with an unusual octagonal church which was added to the 15th-century tower in 1759. In 1762, jilted Hannah Baddaley flung herself from the precipice known as Lover's Leap, but her voluminous skirts acted as a parachute and saved her.

STYAL

CHESHIRE. VILLAGE OFF B5166, 1 MILE (1.5KM) N OF WILMSLOW

This attractive model village was built to house workers at nearby Quarry Bank Mill, a large cotton mill. The National Trust owns the mill, village and woodlands.

Quarry Bank Mill & Styal Country Park

QUARRY BANK MILL, OFF B5166, 1½ MILES (2.5KM) N OF WILMSLOW
TEL: 01625 527468

Quarry Bank Mill is a Georgian cotton mill now restored as a working museum of the cotton industry and powered by a waterwheel. There are galleries illustrating all aspects of the textile process – spinning, weaving, dyeing etc – and the role of the founders (the Gregs), pioneers of the factory system. Other attractions include the factory 'colony' near by with its shop, cottages and chapels. The original 1790 apprentice house, which was the home of young pauper apprentices, is fully restored and open to visitors. The garden is laid out in Victorian 'utilitarian' style, growing fruits, vegetables and herbs using the same methods as 150 years ago. The museum is still developing, therefore displays and facilities are changed from time to time. The mill is set in a lovely valley and there are pleasant walks through woodland or by the deep ravine of the River Bollin. Work is underway to restore steam power with an 1840s beam engine. Events are planned throughout the year.

Open all year, Apr–Sep daily, Oct–Mar most days.

TADDINGTON

DERBYSHIRE. VILLAGE OFF A6, 5 MILES (8KM) W OF BAKEWELL

A village at the head of Taddington Dale. At the top of the village is the 14th-century church, with an ancient cross shaft in the churchyard. Well-dressing takes place in August.

This hamlet is situated in the picturesque Goyt Valley. The Church of St James (which was once dedicated to St Leonard) has a monument to Michael Heathcote (died 1768), 'Gentleman of the Pantry and Yeoman of the Mouth' to George III.

Thorpe is located where the River Manifold joins the River Dove, which forms the border with Staffordshire. The conical hill of Thorpe Cloud, 942ft (187m) high, guards the entrance to dramatic Dovedale.
(See also Cycle ride: The Manifold Track and Ilam, page 56.)

Situated between limestone dales and uplands, Tideswell has a large cruciform church known as the 'cathedral of the Peak', which was built in the 14th century over a period of 75 years, and is topped with a pinnacled tower. Musical events are held in church. Well-dressing takes place in June.

A small gritstone village, with weavers' cottages from the 18th- and 19th-century cotton industry, overlooking Bottoms Reservoir in the Longdendale Valley. Tintwistle is close to the border with Cheshire.

A beautiful estate village of stone houses with Jacobean Tissington Hall, a church with a Norman tower, and a triangular green. The Tissington Trail is near by.
(See also Cycle ride: The Tissington Trail from Ashbourne to Hartington, page 78.)

TAXAL
DERBYSHIRE. HAMLET OFF A5002, 1 MILE (1.5KM) S OF WHALEY BRIDGE

THORPE
DERBYSHIRE. VILLAGE OFF A515, 3 MILES (5KM) NW OF ASHBOURNE

TIDESWELL
DERBYSHIRE. SMALL TOWN ON B6049, 6 MILES (10KM) E OF BUXTON

TINTWISTLE
DERBYSHIRE. VILLAGE ON A628, 2 MILES (3KM) N OF GLOSSOP

TISSINGTON
DERBYSHIRE. VILLAGE OFF A515, 4 MILES (6KM) N OF ASHBOURNE

Tideswell in summer

THE TISSINGTON TRAIL FROM ASHBOURNE TO HARTINGTON

*T*he Tissington Trail is a straightforward route along a disused railway line, incorporating tarmac and rolled shale surface, suitable mainly for hybrid mountain bikes. There are lovely views of the limestone countryside of the White Peak – and despite that name, the route is fairly level, making this route a leisurely traffic-free ride that can be enjoyed by all the

INFORMATION

Total Distance
26 miles (42km), with 22 miles (35.5km) off-road

Difficulty
Easy

OS Map
Landranger 1:50,000 sheet 119 (Buxton, Matlock & Dovedale)

Tourist Information
Ashbourne, tel: 01335 343666;
Peak National Park Office,

Bakewell, tel: 01629 816200

Cycle Shop/Hire
Peak Cycle Hire, Ashbourne, tel: 01335 343156

Nearest Railway Station
Uttoxeter (12 miles/19km)

Refreshments
Pubs and cafés in Ashbourne and Hartington; cafés on the Trail at Tissington and Alsop; several picnic spots along the Trail

START
Ashbourne, just outside the Peak District National Park, is situated at the crossing of the A515 and A52, between Derby and Stoke-on-Trent. Park in the car park north-west of the town centre on Mappleton Lane.

Spring greenery, Tissington Estate

DIRECTIONS

1. From the car park, join this – the southern – end of the Tissington Trail, and set off northwards towards Tissington. For the first 2 miles (3km) the route is mainly lined with trees, offering great places for woodland birds. After about 3 miles (5km) at Thorpe, there is a pleasant picnic site. You are now inside the southern boundary of the Peak District National Park. Continue along the route and cross over the A515 to reach the village of Tissington.

2. Bear left to explore Tissington. Facilities here include toilets and a café. Return to the Trail and continue northwards. After about 1 mile (1.5km) the trees open out

to reveal the rolling Derbyshire landscape with its appealing drystone walls, its valleys and hills. Pass a hotel on the left, and reach the car park at Alsop.

3. From here a footpath lies eastward to the little hamlet of Alsop en le Dale, or you can explore the lane westward which leads to the northern tip of scenic Dovedale. Return to the Tissington Trail and continue northwards, passing under the A515 and following the curve of the hill. Pass over a minor road and continue through a cutting, with the little hill of Johnson's Knoll on the left. Stay on the trail passing the settlements of Greenhead and Biggin on the left. Pass under a minor road and through a cutting

The Trail makes use of a former railway line

to reach the car park just before the B5054.

4. The Tissington Trail continues northward to Parsley Hay and beyond, but leave the route here and turn left along the B5054 for the steep descent into Hartington. Explore here before retracing your route back up the hill. Rejoining the Tissington Trail turn south. Retrace the outward route back into the centre of Ashbourne. Note: the Tissington Trail is used not only by cyclists but also by walkers and horse riders, and consideration must be given to other trail users.

PLACES OF INTEREST

Ashbourne

The old market town has always been an important commercial centre, at the point where so many routes meet, and its prosperity may be seen among the splendid Georgian buildings of Church Street.

Ashbourne is perhaps most famous for its very own annual

The Green Man sign at Ashbourne

Shrovetide Football game, which is played over a three-mile 'pitch', when the Up'ards (those inhabiting the ground north of the Henmore Brook) take on the Down'ards (those living to the south).
(See also page 4.)

The Tissington Trail

The former railway line runs for 13 miles (21km) from Ashbourne to Parsley Hay, where it links up with the scenic High Peak Trail.

By the pond at Tissington

The original railway was constructed towards the end of the railway boom in 1899, and never ran at its hoped-for capacity. However, today its trail provides a popular route for walkers and cyclists through the limestone scenery of the southern Peak District.

Tissington

The attractive village which gave its name to the Tissington Trail is synonymous with the old Derbyshire tradition of well-dressing, when elaborate floral designs are created, usually with a religious theme, to decorate local wells. The ceremony at Tissington is one of the oldest and dates back to the middle of the 14th century; there are five wells here, including a 'children's' well, and dressing takes place around Ascension Day.

(See also page 77.)

Hartington

This pleasing village is built around an unusually wide square, and is set in some of the loveliest scenery in Derbyshire. The limestone landscape is littered with prehistoric burial sites and ancient earthworks, and there are signs too of the lead-mining which once made the village prosperous.

(See also page 42.)

The pretty village of Hartington with its medieval church

WHAT TO LOOK OUT FOR

Disused railway tracks can be a stable refuge for all sorts of wildlife, and the Tissington Trail is no exception. Look out particularly for wild flowers, including meadow cranesbill, wild thyme, harebell and even occasional patches of heather – a reminder that this area was once covered by heath. Look out for birds, too, including wheatears and springtime flocks of lapwings.

UPPERMILL
GREATER MANCHESTER. VILLAGE ON A670, 5 MILES (8KM) E OF OLDHAM

The largest of Saddleworth's picturesque villages, on the moor. Saddleworth Museum is based in the old mill building next to the Huddersfield Canal (see below).

Saddleworth Museum & Art Gallery
HIGH ST
(ON A670)
TEL: 01457 874093 & 870336

There is something for everyone at Saddleworth Museum, which vividly brings to life the history of the Saddleworth area – a piece of Yorkshire stranded on the Lancashire side of the Pennines. Woollen weaving is the traditional industry, displayed in the 18th-century weavers' cottage and the Victoria Mill Gallery. The Victorian Rooms – parlour, bedroom, kitchen, scullery and privy – show the life of one Saddleworth family in the 1890s. Local history, farming, transport and vintage vehicles are also featured. In the art gallery, exhibitions change monthly. Various events are held during the year.
   Open all year, daily. Closed 25 Dec.

WARSLOW
STAFFORDSHIRE. VILLAGE ON B5053, 7 MILES (11KM) E OF LEEK

Stone cottages and an 18th-century church with good furnishings stand at the heart of this moorland village. The chancel of the Church of St Lawrence contains windows by William Morris.

WETTON
STAFFORDSHIRE. VILLAGE OFF A515, 7 MILES (11KM) NW OF ASHBOURNE

An exposed moorland village of old stone cottages with Castern Wood Nature Reserve and dramatic Thor's Cave overlooking the Manifold Valley near by. There are splendid views from the village.
   (See also Cycle ride: The Manifold Track and Ilam, page 56.)

The Huddersfield Canal at Uppermill

THE SADDLEWORTH MORRIS MEN AND THE RUSHCART PROCESSION

The origins of rushcarts in Saddleworth are uncertain; one school of thought is that the festival was a pre-Christian celebration. What is known is that there have been rushcarts in the Saddleworth area since the 17th century at least. At one time, each village and hamlet would build a rushcart and there are records of up to 13 rushcarts at Heights Church overlooking Delph.

The Saddleworth Morris Men's 50th anniversary rushcart

The rushes were used to cover the earthen floor of the church where they would lie until the following spring. They provided insulation and, by the process of composting, warmth for the congregation during the cold Pennine winters. At the Parish Church of St Chad in Uppermill the custom continued until a visit by Bishop Law in 1821, when he told the churchwarden, 'Why, sir, your church is literally a stable with rushes instead of straw'. Following this, the church was partly rebuilt with a stone flagged floor and the rushes, which were still carried in rushcarts, were sold off as animal bedding.

Rushcarts were built during the Wakes when local mills were closed for the annual holiday. With the arrival of the railway, however, more people took advantage of cheap excursions and the popularity of the rushcarts waned. There was a revival of the festival in Uppermill when in 1903, after an absence of 12 years, a rushcart was built in the yard of the Commercial Hotel by 'Sailor' Tweedale, but the custom eventually died out just after World War I.

The current Saddleworth Rushcart was revived by Saddleworth Morris Men in 1975 following extensive research by Peter Ashworth, the founder member of Saddleworth Morris Men. He consulted the older members of the community and obtained information of the early 20th-century rushcarts. The cart is still built behind the Commercial Hotel using rushes cut from the surrounding moors. Two tons of rushes are stacked on a two wheeled cart to a height of around 15ft (4.5m) and topped with a rowan branch.

Saddleworth Rushcart is held on the second Saturday after 12 August when the cart is decorated with heather and the front is covered by a colourful banner. One of the Saddleworth men climbs to the top and sits astride the tower of rushes to be pulled round the major villages of the parish by 170–200 morris men from all over the country. In the evening there is a country dance in the Civic Hall. On Sunday, the

rushcart is taken to St Chad's for the Rush-bearing Service when some rushes are mixed with fragrant moorland herbs and are spread in the aisles to symbolise their original use. After the service, there are displays of Morris Dancing followed by competitions to find the Best Musician, the Best Clog-stepper (clog dancer), the Best Gurner (face puller), the Worst Singer (!) and the Champion Wrestler of the morris men present.

A processional dance performed by Saddleworth Morris Men

*A lovely walk from the village of
Wetton, which rises to the
spectacular entrance of Thor's Cave,
named after the Norse god of thunder,
before descending into the beautiful
Manifold Valley.*

Grid ref: SK109552
INFORMATION

The walk is 3 miles (5km) long.
Varied terrain, with one steep
descent and ascent and an easy,
level section on a former railway
track; a few stiles.
Some road walking on quiet
lanes.
Dogs should be kept on leads.
The Olde Royal Oak in Wetton
has a family room.
Picnic site at Weag's Bridge.

Toilets at car park.

START

Wetton village is on a minor road
1 mile (1.5km) west of
Alstonefield and about 6 miles
(9.5km) north of Ashbourne. The
National Park car park lies on the
southern edge of the village.

DIRECTIONS

1. From the car park turn right,
walking away from the village
centre towards Grindon. Take the
first turning right, signposted
'Wetton Mill', then in 200yds
(183m) turn left at the sign
'Wetton Mill/Manifold Valley'.
After about 30yds (27.5m), turn
off the road to the left, following a
walled green lane, signposted
'Concessionary path to Thor's
Cave', for ¼ mile (0.5km).

2. After crossing a stile by a gate,
continue along a track for another
50yds (45m), then turn right over
a stone stile and follow the
waymarked path down the field,
to the right of the hill. At the end
of the second field cross a fence
stile and descend on a sometimes
slippery path to the cave, which
is prominent in the limestone crag
above (take particular care with
children here). After visiting the
cave (superb views), descend via
the steep flight of steps (slippery
after rain) to the valley.

3. Cross the footbridge, turn left
and follow the Manifold Track
(not signed) along the winding,
wooded course of the river, which
is to your left for about ¼ mile
(0.5km) to Weag's Bridge. Turn
immediately left over the bridge
and follow the minor road which
shortly climbs steeply uphill for
about ½ mile (1km). After crossing
a cattle grid, turn left over a stone
stile and ascend across a field,
keeping the wall to your left.

4. At the top of the field turn left
on to a lane, which will bring you

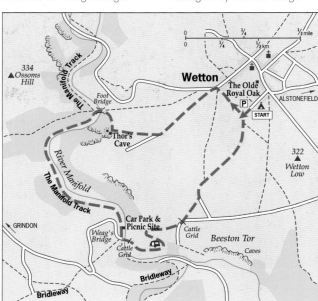

back to the start point in about
½ mile (1km).

Thor's Cave

Set 300ft (91.5m) above the
Manifold Valley in a huge
limestone cliff, Thor's Cave was
inhabited by prehistoric man and
evidence found here suggests that
the cave was occupied more or
less continuously until Romano-
British times.

The Manifold Track

This leisure route uses the line of
the former Leek and Manifold
Light Railway, which ran on a
narrow gauge track up the valleys
of the rivers Hamps and Manifold
for 30 years from 1904. It
catered mainly for local traffic,
particularly taking milk from the
Staffordshire hills to the Potteries,
and featured delightful primrose
yellow carriages and unique tank
engines, originally designed for
use in India.

*The mouth of the spectacular
Thor's Cave*

WHAT TO LOOK OUT FOR

*The River Manifold disappears into underground channels during the summer months, reappearing
at Ilam, several miles downstream. This is a common feature of rivers running across the limestone
rock in this part of the Peak District, which is known as the White Peak because of the
predominant colour of the rock. If you look carefully at the rocks in the many drystone walls which
criss-cross the landscape, you will find the fossils of sea lilies and shells, laid down in a shallow,
tropical sea some 300 million years ago.
Early purple orchids and meadow cranesbill will be found in summer by the path into the valley
from Wetton, and in May and June listen for blackcaps and willow warblers.*

WILDBOARCLOUGH
CHESHIRE. VILLAGE OFF A54, 5 MILES (8KM) SE OF MACCLESFIELD

A remote hamlet in the Pennine foothills, surrounded by sheep farms. There are panoramic views from the top of Shutlingsloe Hill.

WINCLE
CHESHIRE. HAMLET OFF A54, 5 MILES (8KM) SE OF MACCLESFIELD

A pretty hamlet in the Dane Valley on the edge of the National Park. The Ship Inn is a popular country pub.

WINSTER
DERBYSHIRE. VILLAGE OFF B5057, 4 MILES (6.5KM) W OF MATLOCK

An attractive gritstone village, once a lead-mining centre and market town, with many 18th-century houses. Other notable buildings include the 17th-century Dower House and the 17th- to 18th-century Market House, a delightful building of stone arches, now filled in, and an upper storey of brick with stone dressings. The building, bought by the National Trust in 1906, is now an information room.

WIRKSWORTH
DERBYSHIRE. TOWN ON B5023, 4 MILES (6.5KM) S OF MATLOCK

This small market town was once the centre of the lead-mining industry, and the Barmote Court which regulates the industry still meets twice a year in the 19th-century Moot Hall. The area surrounding Wirksworth is still extensively used for quarrying, with the nearby National Stone Centre demonstrating many everyday uses for stone. At the heart of the town is the sloping market place, and the nearby heritage centre illustrates aspects of the town's past in its displays. Substantial 17th- and 18th-century houses contribute to the pleasant townscape, with some earlier buildings including 16th-century Gell's Bedehouses. The impressive cruciform church dates mainly from 1272, its 13th- and 14th-century tower topped by a lead-covered spike. The

Wincle church and schoolhouse

clerestory was added and the east end altered in the 19th century, while an Anglo-Saxon coffin lid and Norman fragments give clues to an earlier building.

Elizabeth Evans, George Eliot's aunt, is buried in the churchyard, and the novelist used the town as 'Snowfield' in *Adam Bede*. Arkwright's 1770s Haarlem Mill, and Providence Mill of about a century later, bear witness to the town's textile history.

Wirksworth Heritage Centre
CROWN YARD
ON B5023 OFF A6
TEL: 01629 825225

The Centre has been created in an old silk and velvet mill. The three floors of the mill have interpretative displays of the town's past history as the hub of a prosperous lead-mining industry. Each floor offers many features of interest including a computer game called 'Rescue the injured lead-miner' and a mock-up of a natural cavern. The lifestyle of a quarryman in the early 1900s is recreated in the Quarryman's House Place. Some unusual local customs such as tap dressing and 'clypping the church' are explained. There are also workshops showing the skills of cabinetmakers and a silversmiths. If you visit Wirksworth during the Spring Bank Holiday, you can also see famous well-dressings.

Open all year, most days.

YOULGREAVE
DERBYSHIRE. VILLAGE OFF
B5056, 3 MILES (5KM)
S OF BAKEWELL

Explore Derbyshire in the summer months and you are likely to come across the ancient art of well-dressing. It is not just wells that are dressed nowadays. In Youlgreave the public taps are adorned with these elaborate pictures made of flowers, mosses, seeds and cones, as well as its fountain.

This is an attractive old lead-mining village high up in limestone Peakland. Its main street straggles along the hillside above the River Bradford, dominated by the big battlemented, pinnacled and gargoyled tower of the Norman church, one of the best in the area. Inside, it is all sturdy columns and capitals. The 13th-century font uniquely has two bowls, and there is a panel of similar date showing a Norman in a long robe. The excellent monuments include an effigy of Thomas Cokayne (died 1488) remarkable for its tiny size. The church was restored in 1870 by Norman Shaw and has stained-glass windows by Burne-Jones and Kempe. There are some good 18th-century stone houses near by, and to the west are Old Hall Farm (1630) and Old Hall (1650), both lovely hall houses.

The parish register for 1615 describes 'the greatest snow which ever fell upon the Earth within man's memorye'. It lasted from January to May. Drifts covered walls and hedges and people went about 'without sight of any earth eyther upon hilles or valleys'. On Kinder Scout 'uppon May day in the morning, instead of fetching flowers, the youthes brought flakes of snow which lay above a foot deep uppon the moores and mountaynes'. In the Peaks of Derbyshire, nature still takes the leading role.

The area is rich in prehistory and 2 miles (3km) west of the village is Arbor Low, a neolithic stone circle, similar to but smaller than Stonehenge and Avebury. Its stones lie flat, in a circle about 250ft (76m) in diameter.

Youlgreave's Norman church

LISTINGS

ACTIVITIES

Angling

Fishing can be arranged on the rivers of the Peak District and day tickets are required for fishing the reservoirs. Contact the local Tourist Information Centres or tackle shops for details.

Caving and Pot-holing

Local outdoor activity centres arrange trips to various caves in the area where you can explore the fascinating world that exists below ground. Alternatively, visit one of the impressive show caves – Poole's Cavern at Buxton, the Blue John Cavern at Castleton and the Heights of Abraham at Matlock Bath are just a few which offer guided tours suitable for families.

Riding and Trekking

An ideal way to explore the glorious scenery of the Peak District is to book a riding or trekking trip with a local stables. These are usually taken by the hour, half-day or a whole day.

Specialist activities

Abseiling, orienteering, field studies, climbing, boulder and gorge scrambling are just some of the exciting activities to choose from. Contact the local outdoor activity centres.

Walking

There are over 1,600 miles (2,574km) of public footpaths and other areas accessible to walkers in the Peak District. The Tissington Trail and The Manifold Track are ideal for families as they offer easy walking on level tracks. Bakewell, Buxton, Castleton, Cromford and Wirksworth organise town walks led by a Blue Badge Guide; the National Park produces a leaflet giving details of walks led by local rangers, and there are guided walks through the Lathkill Dale National Nature Reserve.

Bakewell Circular Walk

This is a figure-of-eight route making two 50-mile (80-km) circular walks through the Peak National Park starting and finishing at Bakewell.

The Brindley Trail

Runs for 61 miles (98km) from Buxton to Stoke-on-Trent.

The Gritstone Trail

Runs for 18 miles (29km) from Lyme Park in Cheshire to Rushton Spencer in Staffordshire where it joins the Staffordshire Way.

The High Peak Trail

Starts at Wirksworth and quickly climbs on to high ground where it meets the Tissington Trail at Parsley Hay.

The Limestone Way

Runs for 26 miles (42km) from Matlock to Castleton.

The Manifold Track

Follows the route of the Leek and Manifold Light Railway north along the Manifold Valley and river from the A523 near Waterhouses.

The Monsal Trail

Runs for 8½ miles (14km) from Blackwell Mill Junction near Buxton to Coombs Viaduct near Bakewell.

The Pennine Way

Runs for 256 miles (412km) from Edale to Kirk Yetholm, just over the border in Scotland.

The Sett Valley Trail

This trail runs for 2½ miles (4km) from New Mills to Hayfield.

The Tissington Trail

Runs for 17½ miles (28km) along part of the old Ashbourne–Buxton railway and the Cromford and High Peak line. The grassy trackway runs alongside Dovedale from Ashbourne, then climbs to join the High Peak Trail near Parsley Hay for the last mile of the route.

Well-Dressing

Well-dressing, the most famous and picturesque of Peak District traditions, takes place in many villages from May to September. Eyam, Hope, Tideswell, Tissington and Youlgreave are among the villages which continue this custom, which is now a major tourist attraction.

CONTACTS AND ADDRESSES

USEFUL ADDRESSES AND NUMBERS

Peak National Park Information Centres

Peak National Park Head Office
Aldern House, Baslow Road, Bakewell
Tel: 01629 816200

Castleton, Castle Street
Tel: 01433 620679

Edale, Fieldhead
(on right side of road from Edale Station to village)
Tel: 01433 670207

Fairholmes (Derwent Valley)
Tel: 01433 650953

Hartington Old Signal Box
(on the Tissington Trail, 1½ miles from Hartington village)
(no telephone)

Langsett, Langsett Barn (south of Penistone)
Tel: 01226 370770

Torside (Longdendale Valley)
(no telephone)

Information Centres are closed over Christmas and some at lunchtimes.

OTHER ADDRESSES

English Heritage, Hazelrigg House, 33 Maresfair, Northampton
Tel: 01604 730320

English Nature, Manor Barn, Over Haddon, Bakewell
Tel: 01629 815095

National Trust, East Midlands Regional Office, Clumber Park Stableyard, Worksop
Tel: 01909 486411

TOURIST INFORMATION CENTRES

*Ashbourne
13 Market Place
Tel: 01335 343666

*Bakewell
The Old Market Hall, Bridge Street
Tel: 01629 813227

Buxton
The Crescent
Tel: 01298 25106

Chesterfield
Peacock Information Centre, Low Pavement
Tel: 01246 207777/8

Glossop
The Gatehouse, Victoria Street
Tel: 01457 855920

Holmfirth
49–51 Huddersfield Road
Tel: 01484 687603

Leek
1 Market Place
Tel: 01538 381000

Macclesfield
Town Hall
Tel: 01625 504114

Matlock Bath
The Pavilion
Tel: 01629 55082

Saddleworth
High Street, Uppermill
Tel: 0145787 4093

* Denotes seasonal opening only

INDEX

INDEX

ACKNOWLEDGEMENTS

The Automobile Association wishes to thank the following photographers and libraries for their assistance in the preparation of this book.

ANDY WILLIAMS PHOTO LIBRARY Front cover, main picture
INTERNATIONAL PHOTO LIBRARY Back cover, top
SPECTRUM COLOUR LIBRARY 36/7, 47.

The remaining photographs are held in the Association's own library, (AA PHOTO LIBRARY) and were taken by P Baker Back cover, middle, Back cover, bottom, 11, 16/7, 18/9, 29, 64/5; J Beazley 70; S Beer 35, M Birkett 51, 74, 79, 88/9; D Forss 32, 87; V Greaves 20/1, 58b; J Gregory 83, 85; A Hopkins 7, 8a, 22, 26/7, 30, 38/9, 40/1, 42, 44/5, 48/9, 52/3, 61, 62/3, 66, 68, 73, 76/7, 80a, 81, 91; C Jones 50; J Morrison 15, 60, 82; R Newton 25, 57; A Tryner 6, 9, 54/5, 78; J Welsh 56, 58a, 59; L Whitwam 8b, 12/3, 80b.